THE WORLD'S
FASTEST CARS

THE WORLD'S FASTEST CARS

JOHN McGOVREN

the apple press

A QUINTET BOOK

Published by Apple Press Ltd.,
293 Gray's Inn Road,
London WC1X 8QF

ISBN 1 85076 051 9

This book was designed and produced by
Quintet Publishing Limited
6 Blundell Street, London N7

Art Director Peter Bridgewater
Editor Nicholas Law

Typeset in Great Britain by
Central Southern Typesetters, Eastbourne
Colour origination in Hong Kong by
Universal Colour Scanning Limited, Hong Kong
Printed in Hong Kong by Leefung-Asco
Printers Limited

Contents

INTROD

It is not easy to decide which single country, if any, is the true home of the fast car, as so many countries can put forward a claim, of sorts. On any enthusiast's short list of really fast cars, however, half a dozen makes will inevitably dominate the top places: Ferrari, Porsche, Lamborghini, BMW, Maserati and Mercedes-Benz. Why this should be is probably obvious, even to the layman, but there are other considerations affecting my choice that need some explanation.

Let's start with Italy, a marvellous country of passionate people with an intense love of competition, not only in things sporting but in life in general. They have a long standing addiction to speed, be it of the pedal-driven two-wheel variety, or the powered kind. Italy was the first country in the world to develop a system of high speed inter-city motor roads and that served to filter out the lame, halt and unfit automobiles of the time, leaving only tough and reliable machines to go on to greater things. In the great days of automobile competition Italy was a country that seemed to support more races than there were days on the calendar. The sport of auto-racing, however, could not have developed in Italy without the fullest support of the government, people, and industry. These factors have made sure that, in spite of any other problems, Italians continue to love the fast car.

In recent years Italy has been burdened with a national system of speed limits; at the time of their introduction it was feared that they might prove to be the beginning of a cooling-off of the Italian love affair with speed but after several years there is little evidence of any reduction in this love. The Italians still make fast cars and they still drive fast cars fast!

Neither the Italians nor the Germans believe in the nonsense that speed kills; both appreciate that it is the unskilled driver who does all the damage. They know that if the driver is educated properly, given good equipment to use and good roads on which to use it the end result is not only greater respect for speed but also a deal more fun in using it safely. Italian fast cars have always been among the quickest anywhere for their day and the Italian racing colour of red is still the only *really* appropriate colour for an Italian car — be it a Fiat Topolino or a Ferrari Daytona coupé!

Italians love the automobile with a fervour that only a Latin race could display and their excitement can be recognized as a result of the Italian car itself. Having owned Italian cars as diverse as a 1938 Lancia Aprilia, a 1971 Lancia Fulvia and a 1972 Fiat 130 saloon, I can attest to the fact that each displayed a verve, a *brio* (to use a very appropriate Italian word) that few other cars of the time, if any, could approach. They all cried out to be driven as fast as the road and conditions allowed, yet all retained the secure and sure-footed feel of a real thoroughbred. Such a feeling comes only from an integrity on the part of a car maker who realizes that his products will be used hard — and so makes sure that his cars will not be found wanting.

The automobile designer and engineer in Italy hold a very special place in that country's social strata. They are highly respected — or, in the case of Enzo Ferrari, virtually worshipped — by the ordinary people. This factor alone must have a tremendous bearing on the quality of the Italian fast car. Technical education and the competitive nature of Italian industry throw up great engineers, designers, innovators and managers with great speed. The same background has also created some of the world's greatest competition drivers. To car enthusiasts the world over, names like Pininfarina, Nuvolari, Ascari, Bertone, Giugiaro, Jano, Lamborghini and Agnelli are part of the very fabric of motoring.

Italy not only provided support and enthusiasm for the automobile and its use but also offered one of the most perfect proving grounds for the refinement of the car. Until recently virtually all Italian car production was concentrated in the north, in and around the cities of Turin and Milan. To the north of these lie the mountains, to the west and the south west are the plains. The former test the agility, acceleration, roadholding, steering and braking of any car, while the fast straight roads of the latter, stretching for mile after mile, expose any shortcomings in reliability, durability and stamina. Good streamlining, to use an old-fashioned phrase, originally came about not after development in a wind tunnel but after hard-pressed miles on the plains of Lombardy. The same testing under real road conditions helped prove the supplementary needs of proper seating, efficient controls and even decent ventilation. Add to these the propensity of the typical Italian driver to keep his right foot and the accelerator all the way to the floorboards at each and every opportunity and the end result is a breed of very good, tough, fast cars.

Unlike his German counterpart, the Italian fast car builder doesn't pay too much attention to the export of his products. The overseas sales effort made by Ferrari for instance cannot by any stretch of the imagination be compared to that of, say, Porsche. This *may* be due to the difference in production numbers of each marque but I am more inclined to the opinion

6

that much of the answer lies in the character of each nationality. The Latin temperament holds sacred the knowledge that a Ferrari or a Maserati is so desirable that the rest of the world will beat a path to the gates of Maranello or Modena and beg to be allowed to buy one. German manufacturers are less inclined to such reticence, which may offer a crude explanation for the relative abundance of Porsches in, say, California, compared to a paucity of Ferraris.

This dogged determination on the part of German car makers to sell their products overseas, with proper back-up in the form of good dealers, extensive availability of spare parts and access to well trained technicians, not only contrasts with the Italian approach but also ensures that, in Germany, the profits from bigger sales can be ploughed back into research for the development of still better, faster cars.

These two differing attitudes can be well summed up in a comment I once heard from one of the most astute observers of the whole car business: 'To the Italian the production of a fast car is an art; to the German it is business'.

Of course, while most Germans regard their cars as simply functional, there are also those who love them with a fierce passion. One such is the owner of a chain of butchers shops in the Ruhr. He could afford to indulge in his particular dream car, based on a full-race Porsche 917, with a turbocharged flat-twelve engine which in its racing heyday was reputed to develop 1,200bhp! He wanted to use *his* 917 on the public roads, which meant that it had to be street-legalized, with new glass, different headlights, a quieter exhaust system, road tyres and dozens of other modifications to satisfy the law. He approached the Porsche factory to carry out these modifications but they declined — possibly fearing for his sanity! Undeterred, he asked one of the world's leading Porsche racing preparation companies to do the work. They were only too pleased to help and now, during the long summer months, he enjoys himself by driving the world's one and only street-legal Porsche 917!

This action might be considered wildly anti-social in most countries. In the USA for instance he might eventually have got the whole idea off the ground, but it would be hard to imagine such an enthusiast trying to stay on the right side of the law with a 230mph car on a 55mph highway. In Germany he was not only able to get the work done and make the car legal but he found that his neighbours, and seemingly every other road user, loved it! This example, extreme though it is, of the general attitude to the car in Germany, goes a long way to explaining why many people now think of Germany as the modern home of the fast car.

Germany certainly out-produces Italy in sheer numbers of fast cars per year, so if numbers alone mean anything Germany at least has a strong claim to that distinction — though as we will see, Italy and Germany, while undoubtedly the leading contenders, are by no means the only countries with a claim to stake. The USA, Japan, Britain, France — even Sweden and South Africa — build cars which qualify for inclusion in this exclusive league.

Finally, it is worth a moment to consider the future of the whole concept of the fast car. Italy has had speed limits on its superb network of autostradas for several years, yet fast cars are still rolling out of the Ferrari, Maserati, Lamborghini, and Fiat factories in greater numbers than ever before. There is little hope for the end of the USA's 55mph limit, but American manufacturers are turning back to a performance image. There are limits and legislation throughout Europe and Japan, but still the fast cars are launched, so maybe the imposition of speed limits and other regulations has no real effect. Even in de-restricted Germany it is rumoured that an 80mph speed limit could be in operation by 1988. It is already being discussed at length, but knowing a little of the German character, I for one will believe it when I see it happen,

However they are marketed, there is no doubt that fast cars do still sell, even in situations where it would appear that every possible move has been made to restrict their sale and use. In January, for example, it was confirmed that the US national speed limit of 55mph (in force since 1975) would not be raised to a level more in line with modern cars and conditions, although all the evidence suggests that the restriction doesn't save any appreciable amount of fuel, or even lives. It simply makes life unnecessarily difficult for road users and for law enforcement authorities alike.

Yet the sales of really fast cars in the USA increase every year. In California, a state with arguably the best Highway Patrol authority of any and with one of the most anti-car legislatures of all, sales of Porsches have reached such a level that the marque seems almost as prevalent as the VW Beetle once was!

Whatever the future holds for the fast car as a breed, there are more really fast cars available today than at any other time in the history of motoring and now is the time to look at a stunning collection of them.

GERMANY

The German claim to be the true home of the fast car rests on much the same arguments as Italy's. The *autobahn* idea was originally tried during the 1920s, and not, as many people believe, only after Hitler came to power in 1933. An inner-city motorway, the Avus autobahn, was opened in Berlin in 1921 and, surprisingly, the German railway system built a section of autobahn near Bonn in 1928 for use by the public. The success of these early experiments showed Hitler that such a fast road system was feasible, cost effective and, for the military machine that he was building, vital for the rapid deployment of men, materials and equipment.

Since the turn of the century the German education system has placed great emphasis on technical training and research. The automobile received proper attention, fittingly so in the country of its real origin, and this was reinforced by the nature of the people who designed and built German cars. Among them are numbered innovative personalities like Gottlieb Daimler, Karl Benz, Ferdinand Porsche (who was actually an Austrian) and Felix Wankel. These men brought to their automotive genius that special Teutonic stubbornness recognized in so many aspects of German life, a special ability to grind away at problems until they have been surmounted, even if it should take years of effort.

I first noticed this characteristic during the first of many contacts with the Daimler-Benz company in Stuttgart. During 1967, I was taking photographs in the Untertürkheim factory and being shown around by one of the management. I commented on the high proportion of hand-finishing work in the typical Mercedes-Benz car compared to its nearest British counterpart and on the workers' obviously intense application to their work. The whole factory was literally humming with effort. I was quietly informed that the company knew exactly what was expected from everyone involved with the production of its cars and if that meant, for instance, a 30% increase in the inspection staff then that was what happened. The executive went on to describe the Swabian worker as the best in the world, especially for car manufacture; hard working, loyal, self critical and determined to make the best car possible. There was a degree of arrogance in his attitude but it was a benign arrogance, very much like that to be found at Rolls-Royce! In fact it is actually pride, a feature common to all great engineers whatever their nationality.

Germans do not particularly expect life to be easy (although this attitude has begun to change in the last few years) but in my own experience the majority of Germans take life, work and pleasure very seriously. They work hard at all of them! Efficiency is the path they follow and when it comes to making a fast car they make that too as efficient as they can. Each major German manufacturer approaches this important task in his own way as can be seen later.

One final, vital factor, at least over the last 30 years, that has created Germany's present strength as a car manufacturer is its willingness to reinvest profits in research and

Germany is one of the very few places in the world where unlimited speeds are still allowed on public roads — though even in Germany that freedom is now threatened. A road system designed for high speed transit and a legislature which has not condemned speed itself have allowed German manufacturers to develop unashamedly fast luxury cars such as the BMW 635CSi shown here.

development. The German industry has shown that it will pay top salaries for top men and these are the sort of men who help Germany produce world beating cars. The German driver works his car hard and expects total reliability, which has made sure that only the most durable of cars succeeds in this very demanding market place.

I have already offered reasons why Germany might justifiably consider itself to be today's real home of the fast car. In this chapter I will begin to look at the cars themselves and describe a selection of the fastest German production models and their capabilities.

At the time of writing there are no fewer than 35 different models available from German manufacturers which will exceed the base-line 125mph. Most are available in all European markets and in the USA, but specifications — even availability — do vary with local requirements and most of these descriptions will be based on home market models, which are, of course, the most typical.

PORSCHE 959

Porsche have the unique distinction among the major German makers of being able to claim, accurately, that *all* its models will exceed 125mph! Where better to start then, than with a look at the very latest Porsche model, the 959, which goes on sale in 1985. The first astonishing feature about this Porsche is its price. In Britain, the three model range has a starting price of £111,000, or about twice the cost of either a Ferrari Boxer or an Aston Martin Vantage, with a similar equivalent price in the USA! The three types offered will be a luxury roadgoing version, a sporting model and a pure competition vehicle. The price of the sports and competition types increases by leaps and bounds over the price of the 'basic' luxury model, with the cost of the racing version running comfortably into the telephone number league.

The technical specification of the 959 would not be out of place on a NASA space project. Its body is made of Kevlar, a material more usually found in the bodies of endurance racing or Grand Prix cars. This immensely strong, light and corrosion-resistant material has been formed into a wind-cheating shape with a very impressive aerodynamic drag coefficient, or Cd, of only 0·32 yet weighing only 1,226·5lb. The 959's styling continues the recognizable Porsche theme that can be traced back to the introduction of the 356 series, over 35 years ago. In the writer's eyes it is one of the best looking of all Porsches. The Kevlar body is mounted on a galvanized steel chassis that carries racing type suspension with dual wishbones at front and rear. Twin dampers are fitted all round, and those at the front incorporate dual springs. The driver can adjust both ride height and spring rates from the cockpit even while the car is on the move.

On the 959, Porsche fit magnesium wheels with hollow spokes, which allow the wheel and tyre assembly to be monitored constantly for punctures or structural failure. Not only will a drop in tyre pressure due to a puncture be registered but any crack in the wheel material will also cause a loss of pressure and can also be noted instantly by the driver. The tyres are secured to the wheel rims and in the event of a puncture should give the driver time to slow and stop the 959 with complete safety.

The four-wheel-drive system is electronically controlled, to give optimum traction to the car by varying the front-to-rear drive balance automatically at all road speeds. In typically Porsche fashion this fail-safe arrangement has a manual override to allow the driver to select his own setup should he feel that conditions warrant it.

The mid-engined 959 uses a refinement of Porsche's existing 935/936 racing engines that have been so successful throughout the world in recent years. It is a twin turbocharged 2.85-litre flat-six unit with an intercooler. The cylinder heads feature four valves per cylinder and water cooling. The engine

S P E C I F I C A T I O N	
MODEL/TYPE	PORSCHE 959
ENGINE	FLAT-6, 2,850CC, TURBO
HORSEPOWER	400BHP PLUS
TRANSMISSION	6-SPEED 4-WD
CHASSIS	KEVLAR/STEEL
BRAKES	4-WHEEL DISC
TOP SPEED	190MPH PLUS
ACCELERATION 0–100MPH	UNDER 8 SECS
PRODUCTION SPAN	1985 →

block itself however is air cooled. This engine's power output is rated at a minimum of 400bhp and the 959 will accelerate from zero to 62mph in 4.9 seconds, with a top speed of over 190mph! As with all previous Porsche engines the unit has enormous potential for further development in terms of both performance and refinement, and over the next few years will undoubtedly reach quite staggering power outputs.

Porsche intend to build 200 examples of this car and a further 20 pure competition models will be prepared for racing, by the factory and by selected private owners. All the cars will be left-hand drive and each and every 959 will undoubtedly be sold even before Porsche start to build them!

The 959 is the fastest and most expensive car Porsche have ever offered for the road. Although the shape is clearly related to the 911, the car owes more allegiance to the 935 racers.

PORSCHE 911 TURBO

In descending order of performance the Porsche line-up continues with the 911 Turbo model, which is known as the 930 in North America. This car can accurately be described as the current ultimate expression of the 911 concept, that was introduced way back in late 1964. Progressive improvements over the years have upped the 911's power output from 130bhp to 300bhp! Any doubts, however, as to whether the 911 chassis could really cope with 300bhp had already been allayed by even more powerful racing derivatives and the 911 Turbo has all the necessary refinements to enable it to handle this massive amount of power with ease.

Nevertheless, experience suggests that only a really capable driver, used to handling large numbers of horses, can utilize the remarkable potential of this machine to the full. Over the years, together with the substantial power increases, Porsche have improved the roadholding of their rear-engined cars to the extent that now even with so much horsepower it is both easier and safer to use all the available performance. However, in the case of the 911 Turbo in particular, it would be a very foolish driver indeed, especially on wet, twisty roads, who did not treat his car with a deal of respect. Full throttle in the middle of a wet corner is a sure recipe for landing in the ditch!

Like all the 911 models, the Turbo retains some aspects from its past, in particular, its instruments and heating. As with all air-cooled cars the efficiency of the 911's heating and ventilation system varies with the engine speed — slow running in traffic means that little heat is supplied but fast, high-revs use supplies almost too much heat and finding the best compromise is not easy. The instrumentation of the 911 series lags behind the best examples of today's cars; with the exception of the speedo and rev-counter, the other dials and switches are scattered about the dash, and to a new driver they do not fall to hand easily.

A Porsche, however, is not just about decent heating and instrument layout, it is about quality of construction, value for money, sheer performance and fun. The 911 Turbo may be flawed, but its virtues outweigh its faults by a very wide margin. A top speed of over 160mph, acceleration from zero to 62mph in just 5·4 seconds, fuel consumption of 23·9mpg at a steady 75mph, together with the car's incredibly stable resale value really do put the Porsche 911 Turbo into a very special category.

PORSCHE

S P E C I F I C A T I O N	
MODEL/TYPE	PORSCHE 911 TURBO
ENGINE	FLAT-6, 3,299CC, TURBO
HORSEPOWER	300BHP @ 5,500RPM
TRANSMISSION	4-SPEED MANUAL
CHASSIS	STEEL MONOCOQUE
BRAKES	4-WHEEL DISC
TOP SPEED	160MPH
ACCELERATION 0–60MPH	5.4 SECS
PRODUCTION SPAN	1981 →

Although introduced as long ago as 1975 and based on a series which dates from 1964, the Porsche 911 Turbo is still the fastest accelerating car of any in series production. Its understated, almost mundane looks belie truly stunning performance. Porsche pioneered the use of aerodynamic wings on road cars and, with a car as quick as the Turbo, they are not simply for show.

PORSCHE

PORSCHE 911 CS

For about two-thirds of the price of a Turbo there is a Porsche which, to my mind, offers even better value for money. It is the 911 Carrera Sport, with a top speed only about 10mph down on that of the Turbo, at 152mph, better fuel economy, with 31·4mpg at 75mph and a slightly longer 0–62mph acceleration time of 6·1 seconds. The Carrera Sport is more drivable in all conditions than the Turbo, being less nervous in its manner of going. Its five-speed gearbox (compared to the Turbo's four-speed unit) gives a better spread of ratios, and the car feels better balanced on its improved 1985 suspension. This Porsche model must be *the* car to lay away, like a good wine, except that it is so much fun to use that it would be very difficult to put it into storage!

Like its 1973 predecessor the original 911 Carrera, the 1985 version is an instant classic of its type. Some time ago I drove from Los Angeles to New York in a factory prepared Carrera. By comparison with today's car its suspension was firm to the point of being harsh, there was a complete lack of body sound damping, so the car was pretty noisy, but oh, how it went! Crossing Kansas I came across a 47-mile straight road, an empty road, devoid of traffic, people, even birds. I opened up the Porsche and ran flat out for the whole length of that road. The speedometer needle went right off the scale, at 160mph, and stayed there, speeding up on the down slopes, holding the speed on the upgrades and flat sections. The Carrera was as stable as could be; the steering remained positive, without any suggestion of lightness and at the end of the long straight the brakes came on with complete conviction, stopping the car without drama.

S P E C I F I C A T I O N	
MODEL/TYPE	PORSCHE 911 CS
ENGINE	FLAT-6, 3,164CC, OHC
HORSEPOWER	231BHP @ 5,900RPM
TRANSMISSION	5-SPEED MANUAL
CHASSIS	STEEL MONOCOQUE
BRAKES	4-WHEEL DISC
TOP SPEED	152MPH
ACCELERATION 0–60MPH	6.1 SECS
PRODUCTION SPAN	1984 →

The 911 Carrera Sport may not have quite the top speed or the shattering ultimate acceleration of the Turbo, but without even minimal turbo-lag it is even more responsive to the throttle. This makes it more idiot-proof at and around its very high limits but with quite enough power to reward the highest levels of driver skill.

PORSCHE 928S

After the introduction of the 924 model in 1975, rumours soon began to circulate that it would not be long before Porsche would bring out a super-sports coupé, incorporating all that they had learnt with this, their first front-engined car. Enthusiasts were not to be disappointed, as the new 928 broke fresh ground for Porsche.

All previous Porsche cars except the 924 had been either rear-engined or mid-engined, so the 928 was a new departure with its front-mounted V8. This engine featured an alloy block with the pistons running directly in the cylinder bores without the usual benefit of steel liners, and hydraulic tappets. The 928 also offered the option of an automatic gearbox, made by Daimler-Benz. Like the standard five-speed manual transmission, this unit as used on the 928 was located at the rear of the car in unit with the differential. This feature (which was shared by the 924) provided the 928 with near perfect 50/50 front-to-rear balance, with obvious benefits in ride, handling and braking.

Early road test comments waxed lyrical over the car, its performance and its overall dynamic qualities but suggested that an anti-lock braking system (ABS) could well be applied to the 928 and more performance would not be unwelcome. They also, in the main, went on to declare the automatic gearbox as much better suited to the 928 than the manual component, as it appeared to match the character of the car so perfectly — a surprising comment perhaps, in view of the very sporting nature of Porsche products.

With the S model, which followed soon after, and now the 928S Series 2, it would appear that the original criticisms, minor though they were, have been dealt with. The 1985 928S is generally regarded as one of the very best two-seater high performance cars of all time. Many ordinarily cynical road-testers have gone into raptures over the car, their only criticism being that their bank balance wouldn't allow them to own one!

Technical details of the 928S Series 2 give some idea of the immense care and attention to detail that Porsche lavish in ensuring that lovers of fast cars continue to feel this way about the model. The fuel-injected V8 engine has a compression ratio of 10.4:1 to give excellent thermodynamic efficiency with low fuel consumption and the car's superb aerodynamic shape helps in achieving consumption figures of 26.9mpg at 75mph, even with the four-speed automatic 'box. A peak of 310bhp is developed at 5,900rpm and maximum permitted engine speed is 6,500rpm. The 0–62mph time is a very quick 6.2 seconds and the top speed is 158mph. The Porsche 928S Series 2 is a very fine automobile, albeit a rather expensive one, but ownership costs are reduced to quite reasonable levels largely because the servicing intervals are now 12,000 miles.

PORSCHE

S P E C I F I C A T I O N	
MODEL/TYPE	PORSCHE 928S
ENGINE	V8, 4,664CC, SOHC
HORSEPOWER	310BHP @ 5,900RPM
TRANSMISSION	5-SP/4-SP AUTO
CHASSIS	STEEL MONOCOQUE
BRAKES	4-WHEEL DISC
TOP SPEED	158MPH
ACCELERATION 0–60MPH	6.2 SECS
PRODUCTION SPAN	1980 →

The 928S is widely regarded as a 'softer' Porsche although the 911 types make most cars look relatively tame. The 928 is just different, a great state-of-the-art car in its own right, largely free of the 911's aggressive image.

PORSCHE 944 TURBO

Early in 1985 Porsche announced their latest high performance car, the long awaited 944 Turbo model. The body styling is very little different from the non-turbo 944 and the price was expected to be between that of the 911 Carrera and the 911 Turbo. The 944 Turbo's front-mounted four-cylinder engine produces a claimed 220bhp, enough to propel the car to a top speed of 152mph and cover the 0–62mph run in 6.3 seconds. Fuel consumption should be better than that of the 911 Carrera, but no details had been announced at the time of writing. The car's turbocharger is water cooled, and both an intercooler and engine oil cooler are fitted, displaying again the attention to detail which is a recurring feature of the Porsche way of doing things.

The improvement in performance over the standard 944 can be quickly gauged from a top speed of 137mph, 0–62mph in 8.4 seconds for the 'ordinary' car and very similar fuel economy, which helps to balance the substantial difference in price. On each model of 944 certain common features remain: low-drag aerodynamics, a good balance between performance and fuel economy, high top speed, good handling, steering and braking, remarkably high levels of build, fit and finish — together with an understated appearance that appeals to the appreciative enthusiast.

S P E C I F I C A T I O N	
MODEL/TYPE	PORSCHE 944 TURBO
ENGINE	4-CYL, 2,496CC, TURBO
HORSEPOWER	220BHP @ 5,800RPM
TRANSMISSION	5-SPEED MANUAL
CHASSIS	STEEL MONOCOQUE
BRAKES	4-WHEEL DISC
TOP SPEED	152MPH
ACCELERATION 0–60MPH	6.3 SECS
PRODUCTION SPAN	1985 →

When the Porsche 944 *(below)* was introduced in 1982 it helped bridge a gap between the relatively low-powered 924 and the quick but very expensive 928, which was really more of an executive express. It combined what were essentially the 924's mass-produced shell, with some modification, and half the 928's V8 engine. This 944 Turbo *(left)*, introduced in 1985, takes the car a step further towards 911 performance and the best of all worlds.

PORSCHE

PORSCHE 924

At the bottom of the Porsche performance car list is the 924 coupé, which was introduced by Porsche in 1975, after Volkswagen had commissioned them to design a sports coupé to be built and sold under their own name but then decided to drop the whole project. Porsche could not bear to see what they considered to be an excellent car go to waste and so they undertook to make it themselves. The 924 quickly established itself as a very good introduction to Porsche motoring, in spite of the fact that its four-cylinder engine came originally from the Volkswagen commercial van, a fact which was always noticeable when running at high revolutions, where the unit sounded strained and harsh.

However, as with all Porsches, the 924 has received constant refinement, becoming better with each year of production. Today the 924 is still a marvellous first step towards Porsche motoring pleasure and even at its 1985 price is still very good value for money.

As a group all the Porsche models give quality of handling precedence over ride quality and to some people they may appear to be harsh because of that, but with the kind of performance that a Porsche offers this must be the right compromise for the buyer.

The idea that Germany *may* bring in speed limits for its autobahn system makes it interesting to contemplate the future of a company such as Porsche, which builds nothing *but* high performance cars. Perhaps we can take hope from the fact that the best market for Porsche cars is still the USA in spite of a 55mph national speed limit.

Even the bottom car of the Porsche range, the 924, will reach 125mph and offers all Porsche's engineering skills in a fairly inexpensive package. Unlike several earlier Porsche efforts at producing a low-priced model, the 924 is a notable sales success.

S P E C I F I C A T I O N	
MODEL/TYPE	PORSCHE 924
ENGINE	4-CYL, 2,000CC, SOHC
HORSEPOWER	125BHP @ 5,800RPM
TRANSMISSION	5-SPEED MANUAL
CHASSIS	STEEL MONOCOQUE
BRAKES	DISC FR/DRUM R
TOP SPEED	125MPH
ACCELERATION 0–60MPH	9.5 SECS
PRODUCTION SPAN	1977 →

In recent years BMW have advertised their cars as 'The Driving Machines' and from 1985 as 'The ULTIMATE Driving Machines'. As an owner of two BMWs that well fit this description I can only agree with the factory but add that until the 1985 models, BMWs had to be driven hard to realize their full potential but were notorious for being tail-happy when going fast in wet conditions. For years, published road tests almost always made mention of this characteristic but my own experience suggests that it is only apparent when driving on or about the limits of any BMW's adhesion, certainly at very high speeds and more obviously in bad weather conditions. In those circumstances, as with any car, the driver must be on his toes and alert if he does not intend to land in the ditch!

BMW's subtle differences from their German rivals in this sector of the market, Porsche and Mercedes-Benz, may have something to do with the fact that the BMW plant is in Munich, in Bavaria, while the others emanate from Stuttgart. A BMW is not so clinical as a Mercedes-Benz, nor so quirky as a Porsche, in fact a BMW has a distinct flavour of the Italian in its nature. It is that flair, combined, of course, with German design and engineering qualities, that makes the Munich cars so appealing. Sit in a BMW (especially after sitting in an equivalent Mercedes-Benz) and the first impression is of luxury, with well upholstered, comfortable seats, beautifully presented instruments, and excellent carpeting that cossets the driver and passengers so that they feel they are in a car made by humans and not by robots.

BMW M635CSi

The current top of the league among BMW's performance cars is the M635CSi coupé. For 1985 this new model has received a series of major improvements over the previous, and already excellent, 635CSi machine. The new in-line 3,453cc six-cylinder engine has duplex-chain-driven double overhead cams, four valves per cylinder and a compression ratio raised to 9.6:1, instead of the previous 9.3:1. Maximum power is now 286bhp but the new engine is both lighter and more fuel efficient than the earlier unit. At 75mph, consumption is 32.1mpg for the manual gearbox version, which is a remarkable figure. Digital engine electronics controlling the ignition and fuel supply systems have been programmed to give optimum timing and fuel metering under all conditions of speed, engine temperature, air temperature, barometric pressure and other variables. For such a large car with this kind of performance the M635CSi's paltry appetite for fuel is astonishing.

An ABS, anti-lock braking system, is fitted as standard, increasing the braking performance of the car and allowing it to be utilized at maximum efficiency while retaining full steering effect at the same time.

The ultimate driving machine? BMW Motorsport division's engine and suspension modifications turn the already rapid 635CSi into the incredible M635CSi (below). The heart of the matter is a 286bhp 24-valve version of the superb BMW straight-six engine (opposite).

S P E C I F I C A T I O N	
MODEL/TYPE	BMW M635CSi
ENGINE	6-CYL, 3,453CC, SOHC
HORSEPOWER	286BHP
TRANSMISSION	5-SPEED MANUAL
CHASSIS	STEEL MONOCOQUE
BRAKES	4-WHEEL DISC
TOP SPEED	158MPH
ACCELERATION 0–60MPH	6 SECS
PRODUCTION SPAN	1984 →

One particularly interesting feature of all the big BMWs is the availability of the ZF four-speed automatic gearbox, with its three ranges of operation. With this unit, a small switch selects either 'E', for economy, wherein the car assumes a high set of overall ratios, giving excellent fuel consumption but slightly slower acceleration, 'S' for sports-type driving, where there is a change to a lower set of overall ratios for more rapid acceleration, and a third position allowing the gearbox to be used effectively as a manual transmission. With this gearbox, the M635CSi can improve on its fuel consumption figures quite appreciably, to register 32.5mpg at a steady 75mph and no less than 41.5mpg at 56mph, while top speed is 158mph!

The big BMW coupé is smooth, so very smooth to drive — quiet and comfortable enough for four large adults to cover hundreds of miles in a day and not feel distressed at the end of the journey. The BMW's steering and braking are more than capable of handling any road situation, and even visibility for the driver, often a bugbear with coupés, is excellent. Heating, which used to be less than good, is now very much improved, as is the ventilation system. For customers who have to have four decent seats in their coupé, plus all the dash and glamour of a really fast car there is not much that can hold a candle to the M635CSi BMW. At a price in Britain of £32,195, close to, say, a Porsche 928S or a Ferrari Mondial, it is out on its own as a four-seater — nothing else even comes close to its combination of comfort, safety, style and performance.

BMW M535i

In order to meet the challenge of the new 16-valve Mercedes-Benz 190E 2.3 in the smaller car sector, BMW have introduced their M535i. On paper it has more than enough in its specification to face up to, even to beat, the small Mercedes. A new 3,430cc single-overhead-cam fuel-injected straight-six engine develops 218bhp and gives the BMW a 33bhp advantage, plus a top speed of 143mph. Acceleration from zero to 62mph is also better than that of the Mercedes, with a time of 7 seconds against 7.5 seconds. Even the current price is comfortably less, by nearly one third. Rear seat accommodation is much more generous, with proper legroom for two adults, where the rear quarters of the 190E are rather cramped.

There is a choice of three different gearboxes for the M535i buyer, the BMW five-speed with overdrive unit, a close-ratio Getrag five-speed, or the ZF triple-range switchable automatic box, which is my own preference. Braking is by four-wheel ventilated disc units, with ABS anti-lock control. Power-assisted steering is also standard and in use it is really excellent. Handling is of a very high standard for such a heavy car, with no more of the dreaded BMW habit of snapping into instant oversteer if indiscreet use is made of the throttle. Now, the car remains well under control at all speeds. Like the M635CSi, the M535i is a car for covering long distances, at high speeds in safety and comfort.

S P E C I F I C A T I O N	
MODEL/TYPE	BMW M535i
ENGINE	6-CYL, 3,430CC, SOHC
HORSEPOWER	218BHP
TRANSMISSION	5-SP/4-SP AUTO
CHASSIS	STEEL MONOCOQUE
BRAKES	4-WHEEL DISC
TOP SPEED	143MPH
ACCELERATION 0–60MPH	7.1 SECS
PRODUCTION SPAN	1984 →

M-style engineering and cosmetic packaging turn BMW's originally rather staid 5-series saloon into the road-burning 143mph M535i, a Bavarian wolf in wolf's clothing. In this guise the comfortable five-seater will seriously embarass many out-and-out sportscars.

BMW B9

The rapid Alpina C-cars are based on the 3-series BMW, the German manufacturer's small saloon, for owners who want more performance in the same compact package — yet they are far more than just another tuned BMW.

Alpina, the most respected of the many companies which tune and otherwise modify BMWs, is based in the village of Buchloe — not far from BMW's own headquarters in Munich. The company was established in 1965 by Burkard Bovensiepen, a large, amiable man who is a wine connoisseur as well as being a car manufacturer — the only manufacturer in the world officially sanctioned by BMW to produce versions of its cars, sold worldwide as Alpina BMWs. For many years, Alpina and BMW have co-operated closely in developing both road and racing cars, with many impressive wins including the prestigious European Touring Car Championship.

Unlike most, Alpina do not simply bolt on more engine power, but completely re-engineer the basic car with modified suspension, brakes, aerodynamics and interior fittings. Alpina offer virtually any level of modification desired on any of BMW's range and the 3-series based C-cars are the company's biggest sellers. The first was the C1, based on the BMW323i but with a much modified version of the 2,316cc six-cylinder engine. An increase in power output from 150 to 170bhp gave substantially improved performance, matched by very effective suspension changes.

The C2, the newly introduced successor to the C1, is even quicker, with a top speed of 133mph with the close-ratio five-speed Getrag sports gearbox and will accelerate from zero to 60mph in 6.6 seconds. With the 'overdrive' manual gearbox and a higher final drive, the C2 will top 140mph — but at the expense of some of its sparkling acceleration. The excellent four-speed ZF automatic gearbox is an interesting third option.

This level of performance is achieved by using a 2,490cc engine derived from the BMW525 Eta, with special Alpina cylinder head and crankshaft (both based on 323i parts) and Bosch LE Jetronic fuel injection. This is good for a supremely smooth and flexible 185bhp but the C2 is also capable of averaging some 25mpg — helped substantially by the Alpina-designed aerodynamic additions, notably the deep front air-dam. To cope with the extra urge, Alpina also fit progressive rate suspension with Bilstein gas-filled shock absorbers, a limited-slip differential and 195/50 VR16 Pirelli tyres on handsome Alpina alloy wheels. Surprisingly, an ABS anti-lock system is not deemed necessary on the servo-assisted all-disc brakes — which are standard 323i components.

Among the many companies which tune BMWs for road and track use, Alpina is probably the best known — and in racing terms the most successful. Their C1, and C2, which replaced it recently, are both based on the compact 3-series.

S P E C I F I C A T I O N	
MODEL/TYPE	**ALPINA BMW C2**
ENGINE	**6-CYL, 2,492CC, SOHC**
HORSEPOWER	**185BHP @ 6,100RPM**
TRANSMISSION	**5-SP/4-SP AUTO**
CHASSIS	**STEEL MONOCOQUE**
BRAKES	**4-WHEEL DISC**
TOP SPEED	**133MPH**
ACCELERATION 0–60MPH	**6.6 SECS**
PRODUCTION SPAN	**1985 →**

BMW

BMW 745i

Before leaving the really fast current BMWs, mention must be made of a car available only in Germany, the 745i, a 3.5-litre turbocharged 7-Series car. Luxuriously appointed, with an on-board computer, ABS braking, very high levels of trim and equipment, this car is a match for anything else on Germany's high speed autobahns. I tried one on a recent visit to Munich, in the most awful winter weather conditions, with heavy snow and bad visibility, but even so the car impressed greatly. The engine's performance was sensational; completely free of the dreaded turbo-lag, it urged the big, heavy car up to seemingly impossible speeds, yet without any fuss or excessive noise. The ABS braking system handled the very slippery conditions with ease and safety, and the steering further emphasized the overall excellent nature of the car. It is so good as to make the possibility of the appearance of the new 700 series, which *will* be sold outside Germany, something really to look forward to.

On a lower rung of the BMW performance ladder the 735i and the 528i might appear at first to be poor relations for the cars already mentioned, but although somewhat lacking in outright speed they are still cars of very acceptable performance. Their special attraction lies in their lower prices and less prohibitive insurance costs, which for many people may balance out their relative lack of go.

Many German car enthusiasts place BMW second to the cars from Mercedes-Benz but I am happier to think of the Munich cars as simply different, not inferior. Their blend of good looks, performance and attractive interiors, with the normal German qualities of good design and construction, make them a favourite alternative to the Stuttgart cars.

The flagship of the BMW fleet is the large, luxurious 7-series saloon. The turbocharged 745i tops the range in Germany and offers 150mph transport in the grand manner. In other European markets, the normally aspirated 735; (*above and right*) is the quickest of the 7-series.

S P E C I F I C A T I O N	
MODEL/TYPE	BMW 745i
ENGINE	6-CYL, 3,430CC, TURBO
HORSEPOWER	295BHP
TRANSMISSION	4-SPEED AUTO
CHASSIS	STEEL MONOCOQUE
BRAKES	4-WHEEL DISC
TOP SPEED	150MPH
ACCELERATION 0–60MPH	7 SECS
PRODUCTION SPAN	1982 →

S P E C I F I C A T I O N	
MODEL/TYPE	BMW 735i
ENGINE	6-CYL, 3,430CC, SOHC
HORSEPOWER	218BHP
TRANSMISSION	5-SP/4-SP AUTO
CHASSIS	STEEL MONOCOQUE
BRAKES	4-WHEEL DISC
TOP SPEED	135MPH
ACCELERATION 0–60MPH	7.4 SECS
PRODUCTION SPAN	1982 →

S P E C I F I C A T I O N	
MODEL/TYPE	BMW 528i
ENGINE	6-CYL, 2,788CC, SOHC
HORSEPOWER	184BHP
TRANSMISSION	5-SP/4-SP AUTO
CHASSIS	STEEL MONOCOQUE
BRAKES	4-WHEEL DISC
TOP SPEED	127MPH
ACCELERATION 0–60MPH	8.7 SECS
PRODUCTION SPAN	1983 →

Turning to the fastest cars from Mercedes-Benz themselves, however, I must admit to a sneaking regard for the products. Over the last 15 years I have had a professional relationship with the company, and never fail to be impressed when I drive their cars. At the same time, however, I must admit that I have yet to own one! The reason is strictly personal. I actually find it difficult to be enthusiastic about perfection, when, as in the case of Mercedes-Benz cars, it translates to a clinical coldness, an unappealing machine-like efficiency. There is no denying, however, that Mercedes-Benz cars are among the best mass-produced cars available in the world today.

I have selected three cars from Untertürkheim to represent Mercedes-Benz and these are the 380SEC, the 500SEL and the 500SL.

MERCEDES-BENZ 380SEC

The 380SEC is a superb four-seater coupé, well able to carry four adults far and fast, with excellent economy of operation. Its 3,839cc V8 engine produces 204bhp at 5,250rpm, and 225lb ft of torque at 4,000rpm. Maximum speed is 133mph and the 380SEC can maintain this speed all day if necessary! Its 0–62mph time is very good, at 6.4 seconds, but the overall fuel consumption is only average, at 22mpg. In appearance the 380SEC rivals the very good looks of the BMW 635CSi and is without doubt one of the most handsome Mercedes-Benz cars ever made.

In my eyes, the 380SEC is so good looking that anyone thinking about adding any of the increasingly prevalent aftermarket body styling appendages should really think very carefully before changing the standard car's beautifully balanced appearance.

With the elegant 380SEC coupé, Mercedes-Benz show that it is possible to combine performance with style and still retain a strong marque identity—even though the functional simplicity which characterizes the marque is interpreted by some as blandness.

XLB 881X

MERCEDES·BENZ

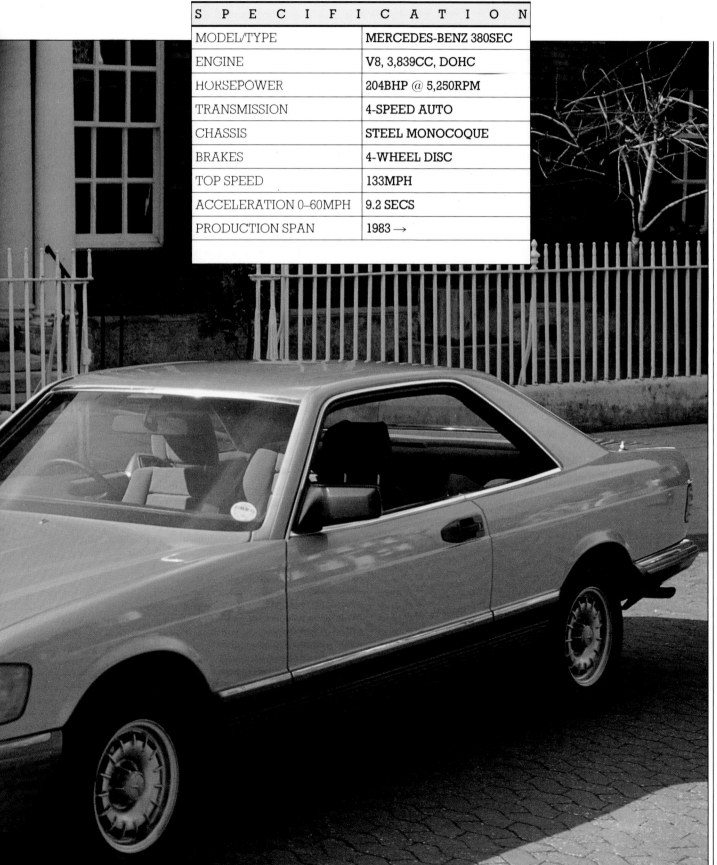

S P E C I F I C A T I O N	
MODEL/TYPE	MERCEDES-BENZ 380SEC
ENGINE	V8, 3,839CC, DOHC
HORSEPOWER	204BHP @ 5,250RPM
TRANSMISSION	4-SPEED AUTO
CHASSIS	STEEL MONOCOQUE
BRAKES	4-WHEEL DISC
TOP SPEED	133MPH
ACCELERATION 0–60MPH	9.2 SECS
PRODUCTION SPAN	1983 →

MERCEDES-BENZ 500SEL

The 500SEL is slightly cheaper than the 380SEC and uses a 4,973cc V8 engine, producing 231bhp at 4,750rpm, which gives the 3,649lb car a top speed of 140mph. The 'S-class' Mercedes-Benz has been one of the most desirable mass produced cars of recent years and the longer-bodied SEL is even more admirable in all respects.

Until the S-class cars came along I thought Mercedes-Benz were without a really good looking model in their range but with the S cars all that has changed. Having looked closely at a number of body styling exercises on Mercedes-Benz models over the last two years I still think that the standard shape is unequalled for looks and proportions.

Fuel consumption for the 500SEL is very slightly better than for the 380SEC, at an average of 23.6mpg and for such a large car it is surprisingly easy to drive quickly. It appears to shrink as the miles fly past, allowing the driver to place the car very accurately on corners. Brakes are discs all round, those at the front are internally ventilated and ABS comes as standard. The transmission is the excellent Mercedes-Benz four-speed automatic and the differential is a limited-slip unit. Suspension is independent all round, with the front having anti-dive characteristics and the rear incorporating anti-squat control.

Mercedes-Benz seats may provide rather a surprise to most people sitting in one of these cars for the first time, as they appear to be both plain and very hard! However, they are anatomically correct in their design and very comfortable even over very long distances. A trip from Nairobi to Mombasa, for instance, through the Tsavo Game Park, over rutted murram tracks in a 280SE left the author feeling no worse than a drive across town.

Irrespective of performance and price, the 500SEL is one of today's great automobiles.

S P E C I F I C A T I O N	
MODEL/TYPE	MERCEDES-BENZ 500SEL
ENGINE	V8, 4,973CC, DOHC
HORSEPOWER	231BHP @ 4,750RPM
TRANSMISSION	4-SPEED AUTO
CHASSIS	STEEL MONOCOQUE
BRAKES	4-WHEEL DISC
TOP SPEED	140MPH PLUS
ACCELERATION 0–60MPH	7.6 SECS
PRODUCTION SPAN	1984 →

MERCEDES-BENZ

The Mercedes-Benz 500SEL is a big car by any standards, but 231bhp and exceptional aerodynamics add up to 140mph performance coupled with surprisingly good fuel economy.

MERCEDES-BENZ 500SL

Mercedes-Benz have always prided themselves on offering a fast convertible that lacked nothing in comfort and whose amenities in no way compromised high performance. The 300SL was a classic example of this type of vehicle and the 'SL' label has come to be applied to many fine sporty convertibles from Mercedes-Benz, a tradition which the latest 500SL continues. The all-alloy 4,973cc V8 engine uses fuel injection, transistorized ignition and hydraulic tappets and produces 231bhp at 5,000rpm. A four-speed automatic gearbox is fitted, as is a limited slip differential. Suspension is as on the 500SEL model and the braking system is also similar.

The 500SL's top speed is 137mph and its 0–62mph time is 7.6 seconds. Fuel economy is an average of 26.5mpg, which makes the 500SL a remarkably economical performance car.

With increasingly restrictive legislation demanding even better crash protection, particularly for the American market, the drophead sportscar came close to extinction in the 1970s but, happily, cars like the 500SL show that the breed has not been stamped out yet.

MERCEDES-BENZ

S P E C I F I C A T I O N	
MODEL/TYPE	MERCEDES-BENZ 500SL
ENGINE	V8, 4,973CC, SOHC
HORSEPOWER	231BHP @ 5,000RPM
TRANSMISSION	4-SPEED AUTOMATIC
CHASSIS	STEEL MONOCOQUE
BRAKES	4-WHEEL DISC
TOP SPEED	137MPH
ACCELERATION 0–60MPH	7.6 SECS
PRODUCTION SPAN	1983 →

AUDI

For many years, Audi made low priced, sensible cars, for the family that aspired to a BMW but couldn't afford one. They were well made in the German manner, rather lacking in character but making up for that by being so well put together and finished. Gradually, Audi's cars became bigger, faster and more sought after by an increasingly prosperous middle class in Europe.

Ten years ago the drive from Cologne to Frankfurt could be undertaken in just under two hours but it took an expensive, fast car to do it. I recently did the same journey in an Audi 80CD and very comfortably took 25 minutes off that time. As a practical measure of the improvement in the current crop of everyday cars this sort of comparison of journey times is of more value than any test track measurement.

Currently there are six Audi cars that can easily exceed 125mph, the 100CD, 2005T, 200T, Quattro, 200 Quattro and the new Quattro Sport. They are all excellent cars but I have zeroed in on the fastest, the 155mph Quattro Sport, not only because it *is* the fastest but also because it incorporates all the latest technology coming out of Audi's base at Ingolstadt. It is also the most expensive car Audi has ever offered to the public, if only a very limited public!

AUDI QUATTRO SPORT

The Audi Sport's capabilities take it out of the merely fast into the super-fast, super-expensive class of car, although it has more than a passing similarity to the more mundane Audi GT coupé. By no means a beautiful car, some have labelled the Sport downright ugly. It sits on a wheelbase that is two inches shorter than that of an Austin Rover Metro, giving the car a short, squat appearance, emphasized by a longer nose to accommodate the intercooler for the turbo unit.

The engine, a new five-cylinder unit, is a benchmark for any turbo installation and marks another step in the progress of

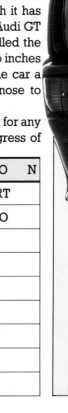

S P E C I F I C A T I O N	
MODEL/TYPE	AUDI QUATTRO SPORT
ENGINE	5-CYL, 2,133CC, TURBO
HORSEPOWER	300BHP @ 6,500RPM
TRANSMISSION	5-SPEED MANUAL
CHASSIS	STEEL/GRP/KEVLAR
BRAKES	4-WHEEL DISC
TOP SPEED	155MPH
ACCELERATION 0–60MPH	5 SECS
PRODUCTION SPAN	1985 →

extracting usable power by means of the exhaust-driven blower. After the introduction of this engine, Audi upped its power in 1980 from 115bhp on carburettors to 130bhp using fuel injection. Use of the turbocharger increased this to 200bhp, with the works rally cars enjoying the benefits of up to 350bhp. This new car has a reliable 300bhp at 6,500rpm even in standard form. Current rally cars have 450bhp, with another 50bhp to come for next year.

The engine installation in the Quattro Sport represents the fourth generation of Audi turbo refinement with its twin overhead camshafts operating four valves per cylinder. The engine, in alloy, is nearly 50lb lighter than the previous cast iron-block engine and is the first all-alloy Audi engine to be offered to the public.

The interior may *promise* to be able to accommodate four people, but in practice the Sport is strictly a two-seater and

AUDI

there is no way that even two small children can be carried in comfort on the rear seats. The body, which is made by Bauer, has boot and roof sections of aluminium reinforced glassfibre, with other body parts using Kevlar material.

One very distinct difference from other Audi models is that the Sport must have the aerodynamic qualities of a house brick, yet sitting on its 225/50VR 15 Pirelli P7 tyres the Sport has all the charisma of the Ferrari GTO.

Never noted as the smoothest of engines, the 2,133cc five-cylinder Audi unit in its latest guise is surprisingly silky, almost as smooth as a BMW six. Real power starts to come in at over 3,000rpm when the familiar turbo 'whoosh', sounding like an astonished gasp from an unsuspecting passenger, takes over. There is also some extra noise from the transmission but its shift quality is not affected and it remains smooth and positive. The brakes are ventilated discs all round and have selectable ABS anti-lock capability. Audi have found that ABS is not necessarily desirable in all driving conditions and in some circumstances can be dispensed with to advantage, so they give a Sport driver the option.

Ride quality is firmer than previous Quattros, to the point where it could almost be described as harsh but, if anything, the roadholding of this car is appreciably better. Steering is also improved to the point where the Sport is easier to drive really fast, much faster than last year's Quattro and with greater relaxation.

Anyone with the equivalent of £60,000 to spend on a car, a two-seater remember, that is in the forefront of the latest technology, with the reliability and durability that comes from German engineering, and which is as safe as any car manufacturer can make it, should look no further than an Audi Quattro Sport.

The stubby and purposeful-looking Audi Quattro Sport (*below left and previous page*) takes the four-wheel drive format of the original Quattro (*below*) a stage further, in a short-wheelbase derivative designed primarily (though not entirely successfully) for rallying.

AUDI 2005T

For the fast car buyer who must have a full five-seater with all the basic advantages of an Audi, the Audi 2005T model may be an ideal choice. The larger 200 body style gives sumptuous accommodation for five large adults with every possible comfort, and the driver has near-sportscar performance to keep him happy. The 2005T has a top speed of 143mph, will accelerate from zero to 60mph in 8.2 seconds and offers overall fuel consumption of just over 19mpg — and this maker's quoted figure for top speed is probably more than a little on the conservative side. The beautifully finished Audi 2005T has only two small causes for criticism. Firstly, it is very expensive within its class and secondly it shares a characteristic with most other Audi's of being too cold and clinical. That however is the price to be paid for a near perfect automobile. If I had to transport five adults a long way in a hurry and in considerable comfort then I can think of few better alternatives than the Audi 2005T.

AUDI (vertical sidebar)

Vorsprung durch Technik—ahead through technology—is the Audi slogan and the 2005T is an excellent example of the company's advanced engineering and stylish packaging.

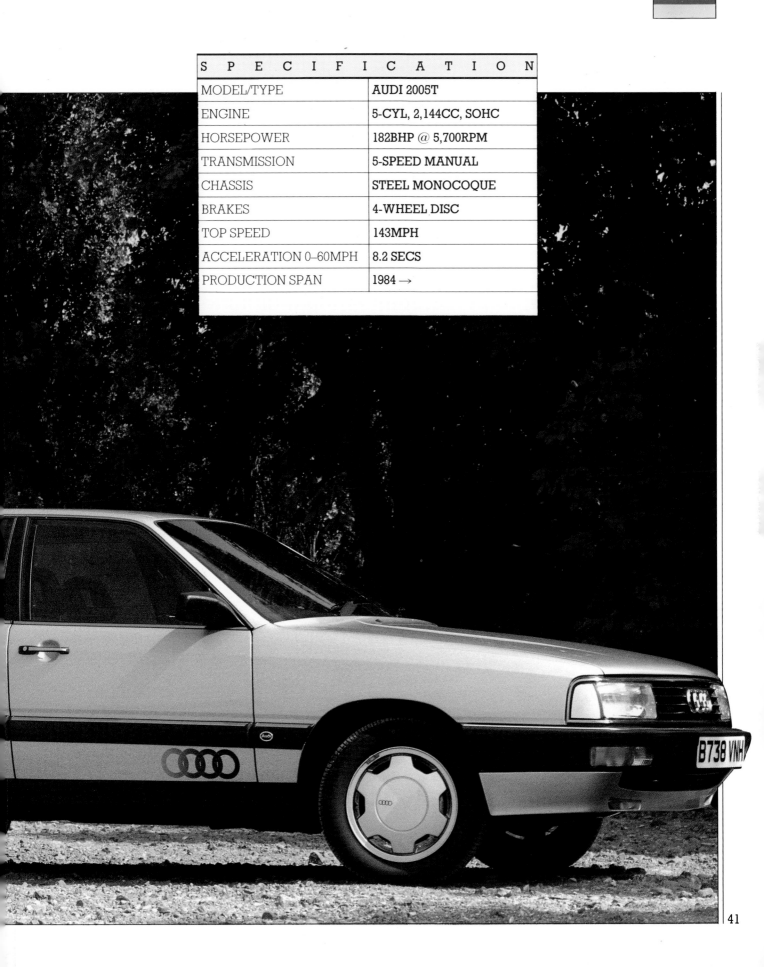

S P E C I F I C A T I O N	
MODEL/TYPE	AUDI 2005T
ENGINE	5-CYL, 2,144CC, SOHC
HORSEPOWER	182BHP @ 5,700RPM
TRANSMISSION	5-SPEED MANUAL
CHASSIS	STEEL MONOCOQUE
BRAKES	4-WHEEL DISC
TOP SPEED	143MPH
ACCELERATION 0–60MPH	8.2 SECS
PRODUCTION SPAN	1984 →

OPEL MONZA GSE

My final selection from the ranks of German fast cars is the excellent but often underrated Opel Monza GSE, which is considerably cheaper than many of its rivals and tremendous value for money. The Monza is a striking looking car that is very well made, most fully equipped, has really excellent road manners and is safe and fast at the same time. The hatchback GSE is able to carry four adults and all their luggage over long distances in great comfort. It is powered by a 3-litre straight-six overhead cam engine developing 180bhp at 5,800rpm and an equally impressive 183lb ft of torque at 4,200rpm. Bosch LE-electronic fuel injection and electronic ignition are fitted and give impressive smoothness and power.

Either a five-speed manual or a four-speed automatic transmission can be ordered with this engine and both options allow the full performance potential to be exploited. With the five-speed manual gearbox, top gear gives 25.5mph per 1,000rpm, a factor that contributes a great deal both to lack of fuss at high speed and fuel economy — which is an impressive 30mpg at 75mph. Four-wheel disc brakes are fitted and these are ventilated at the front and solid at the rear, assisted by a servo and regulated to prevent rear-wheel lock-up in emergency operation.

Light alloy wheels help brake-cooling and enhance the overall appearance of this car, whose top speed is 133mph with the manual gearbox and 130mph with the optional automatic. Its acceleration times are equally good, for the 0–62mph dash the manual takes only 8.2 seconds and the auto-equipped car is just two seconds slower.

With this line-up of fast, or very fast, cars Germany can certainly claim to be the home of some of the fastest cars in the world. It remains to be seen whether the possibility of a national speed limit ever materializes, and if it does what effect it will have on the type of car which German manufacturers build. There are already several short sections of autobahn that are speed restricted, including a notorious downhill stretch between Cologne and Frankfurt that is particularly dangerous in the wet, and in 1975 the government did establish a 50mph overall speed limit to conserve fuel after the Arab/Israeli war. Enormous pressure from the motoring public and from Germany's domestic car makers had the restriction lifted within three months.

It is still difficult to see either an overall speed limit being imposed, or German fast cars slowing down!

OPEL

S P E C I F I C A T I O N	
MODEL/TYPE	OPEL MONZA GSE
ENGINE	6-CYL, 2,969CC
HORSEPOWER	180BHP @ 5,800RPM
TRANSMISSION	5-SPEED MANUAL
CHASSIS	STEEL MONOCOQUE
BRAKES	4-WHEEL DISC
TOP SPEED	133MPH
ACCELERATION 0–60MPH	8.2 SECS
PRODUCTION SPAN	1984 →

The Opel Monza GSE is the top of General Motors' European range and maintains Opel's longstanding reputation as makers of cars with flair. The GSE's smooth fuel-injected straight-six gives the big, well-equipped fastback coupé sparkling performance at remarkably low cost.

ITALY

Italy has long been the home of several famous makers of fast cars, albeit in small numbers, as befits any hand-made product. The very names of these manufacturers, Ferrari, Lancia, Maserati, Lamborghini and Alfa Romeo, conjure up an image of speed and high performance. The rather prosaic name of Fiat can now be added to this list in view of their recently announced Turbo Uno model.

I might reasonably begin this look at Italy by considering Lancia, a company older than all but Fiat of this group of makes and with a proud heritage of building and racing fast cars. In the last 20 years Lancia have suffered badly in the market place, despite enormous financial help from their current owners, the Fiat company. The Lancia has been an engineer's car, and their designers and chief engineers have been household names among Lancia owners. Vincenzo Lancia himself took an enormous pride in his company's products, and right up to his death in 1937, at the early age of 56, he would insist on evaluating on the road every single Lancia model, be it a prototype, research or pre-production car. If it did not at first meet his own very critical standards, the car simply didn't go on to the next stage in its development.

Although a fine racer himself in his early days, Vincenzo believed that sheer horsepower alone was not the way to make a fast car for a customer. Balance was the most immediate obvious feature in all Lancias that were built in Vincenzo's day. Although with the passage of time this characteristic was allowed to become less important, especially after the Fiat takeover, up to the end of the Vincenzo Lancia period all the Turin cars offered the best possible balance between roadholding and horsepower. Chassis performance was essential to the Lancia way of doing things.

It was always possible to find engines with more power per cc than a Lancia from other Italian makers, in particular from Alfa Romeo, and as most people are more instantly impressed by horsepower than by road abilities, Lancias began to appear as less than appealing cars. However, since the end of World War II Lancia models have emerged that must be considered real high performers by any standards.

They include cars like the B20 GT, one of the very first mass production cars properly to qualify for the title of Gran Turismo (and to my mind one of the most beautifully shaped cars of all time). It was also a car with a very honourable record in GT-class racing, scoring a second place in the Mille Miglia in 1951, winning the 1952 Targa Florio, the 1953 Liège–Rome–Liège, the 1954 Monte Carlo Rally and, as late as 1958, winning the Acropolis Rally. Then came the under-financed D50 Grand Prix racing car, which, with more financial backing might have seriously challenged the W196 Mercedes-Benz racing record. Various factory and Zagato-bodied Appias, Fulvias and Flaminias followed.

All were wonderfully responsive cars, lovely to look at and to drive, well engineered but they never really caught the

public's imagination enough to slow Lancia's slide into insolvency. The spectacular Stratos came too late and in any case was not really a proper Lancia in the strictest sense but a Ferrari-engined special built to go rallying, which it did very successfully. In truth, it was more a Fiat exercise than a Lancia one.

To give some idea of the addictive qualities of the marque I can do no better than recount the words of Pininfarina, who after he had styled the lovely Flaminia coupé and had driven thousands of test miles in it, said 'When I die, I want to drive to Paradise in the Flaminia'.

LANCIA THEMA

At last, after years of hovering on the edge of extinction, the name Lancia can again be linked to a car with real performance pretentions, the turbocharged Thema. With a body styled by Giugiaro in co-operation with Lancia's in-house design office, this four-door car looks as ordinary as the Lancias of old. Spectacular body shapes have *never* been the way Lancia have sold their cars (and perhaps that is why they very nearly went out of business). Clean, modern, almost anonymous, would be a good way to describe the Thema's styling but, as always with Lancia, it is what is *under* the bodywork that is important.

The engine of the fastest Thema is a 2-litre four-cylinder, turbocharged, fuel-injected unit delivering 165bhp through a five-speed gearbox. This engine has two counter-rotating balance shafts to smooth out the four-cylinder roughness. The fuel injection is by the Bosch LE-2 Jetronic system, aided by Magnetti Marelli Microplex microcomputer ignition control, which features an 'overboost' arrangement allowing the driver to select, for very short periods, a delay in the turbo wastegate opening which has the effect of increasing torque from a normal 188lb ft to 210lb ft.

The ZF power-assisted rack-and-pinion steering has variable rate characteristics, lowering the ratio at low speeds, to help in parking manoeuvres, and quickening up at higher speeds for more sensitivity. Self-levelling rear suspension and ABS braking are also offered on the turbocharged Thema.

Lancia claim a top speed of 135mph for the car, with a 0–60mph acceleration time of 7.1 seconds. Accommodation for four adults is generous and, in the BMW manner, very luxurious. At speed the old, strained, Fiat 2-litre engine note is absent in the turbo car, but there *is* some wind noise.

Slightly slower than the turbo, at 130mph, is the normally aspirated V6 Thema. It is also a little quieter and requires fewer gearchanges when pressing on fast. This latest Lancia has all the right qualities to restore the marque to its former glories but there is no doubt that the road ahead for the Turin manufacturer is going to be a long hard slog.

LANCIA

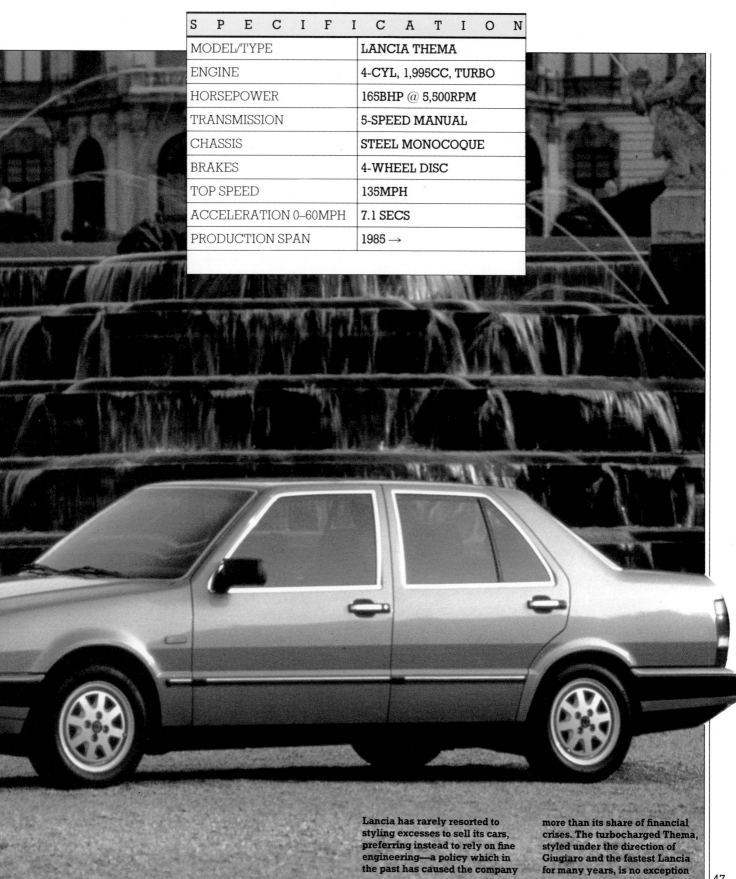

S P E C I F I C A T I O N	
MODEL/TYPE	LANCIA THEMA
ENGINE	4-CYL, 1,995CC, TURBO
HORSEPOWER	165BHP @ 5,500RPM
TRANSMISSION	5-SPEED MANUAL
CHASSIS	STEEL MONOCOQUE
BRAKES	4-WHEEL DISC
TOP SPEED	135MPH
ACCELERATION 0–60MPH	7.1 SECS
PRODUCTION SPAN	1985 →

Lancia has rarely resorted to styling excesses to sell its cars, preferring instead to rely on fine engineering—a policy which in the past has caused the company more than its share of financial crises. The turbocharged Thema, styled under the direction of Giugiaro and the fastest Lancia for many years, is no exception

ALFA-ROMEO GTV-6

The next oldest of these Italian car makers is Alfa Romeo, which, like Lancia, has been teetering on the edge of financial disaster. Also like Lancia, Alfa have a marvellous background in making high performance cars. At the moment they have but one car that qualifies for inclusion in this book, and that is the GTV6. This car follows on from a long line of very fine 2+2-seater GT coupés that goes back to the superb little Bertone-styled Giulietta of the early 1950s. The three-door hatchback GTV6 is powered by the latest in a range of fine Alfa Romeo engines, a 2,492cc all-alloy V6 (of 60° included angle) with twin overhead camshafts, producing 160bhp at 5,600rpm. Bosch L-Jetronic fuel injection is used, together with electronic ignition. A five-speed manual gearbox is mounted at the opposite end of the car, in unit with the differential, and the long gear linkage can sometimes give a less than perfect change.

The GTV6's suspension is rather different from many other fast cars. It is independent at the front, by wishbones and with torsion bars supplying the springing medium, while an anti-roll bar controls sway in cornering. At the rear, however, a de Dion axle is used, with coil springs and an anti-roll bar. This design of axle is not fully independent in the true sense of the word but has the enormous advantage of keeping the rear wheels perpendicular to the road surface at all times, retaining a full tyre contact patch with all the virtues that that gives.

Brakes are disc all round, the fronts having ventilated rotors. Steering is by rack and pinion, without any assistance, and in use none is necessary. The wheels are 15 × 6in light alloy components and the tyres are 195/60HR 15. With the excellent balance achieved by virtue of having the transmission located at the rear of this front-engined car, the GTV6 has wonderful handling qualities. Although the Alfa Romeo has no more power than many of its competitors, it performs as well (and sometimes better) as them because of its balance, road grip and dynamic handling qualities. Above all, it remains very fine value for money in its class.

The Alfa Romeo GTV6 is a car of real character, for better or worse. The attractive coupé has a fabulous V6 engine, exceptional roadholding and handling, a dreadful gearchange and a typically Italian driving position—best suited to long arms and short legs. All the GTV6's shortcomings however are trivial alongside its sheer *brio*.

ALFA-ROMEO

S P E C I F I C A T I O N	
MODEL/TYPE	ALFA-ROMEO GTV-6
ENGINE	V6, 2,492CC, OHC
HORSEPOWER	160BHP @ 5,600RPM
TRANSMISSION	5-SPEED MANUAL
CHASSIS	STEEL MONOCOQUE
BRAKES	4-WHEEL DISC
TOP SPEED	127MPH
ACCELERATION 0–60MPH	8.1 SECS
PRODUCTION SPAN	1983 →

FERRARI

Like Porsche, Ferrari's cars are all capable of more than 125mph and several of them will beat this arbitrary figure by a very large margin. The two most recent, and to date fastest, Ferraris are the Testarossa and the GTO. Both names recall great Ferrari cars from the recent past and Ferrari have used them appropriately enough again on two machines that incorporate all the latest in high performance technology.

Ever since 1950, when Ferrari properly started to make and supply customer cars, as opposed to purely competition machinery, they have given pride of place to their engines. In the vast majority of cases these beautifully crafted power units have followed the overhead-cam V12 layout and plainly show the great influence that Enzo Ferrari himself has on the design philosophy of his company, even though he is now well into his 80s and the customer side of the business is owned by Fiat. As

an ex-racer and racing team manager, his thirst for engine performance dominates his thinking on the Ferrari customer cars. It is not, however, quite as overwhelming as in the past, when the quality of design and performance of a Ferrari road-car engine was streets ahead of the rest of the car, which could often be described as no more than ordinary.

With the coming of 'science' into the closed shop of racing car design nearly 30 years ago, with Lotus's late founding-genius Colin Chapman in the forefront, Ferrari have been forced to take more heed of the other dynamic aspects of their racing cars. As with so many developments at Maranello, these have filtered down to keep their road cars in the vanguard of high performance vehicles. For the record, Ferrari probably make more of the components of their own cars than any other car maker in the world.

FERRARI GTO

Ferrari make no bones about the new GTO and describe it in their own literature as 'The Fastest Ferrari road car ever Built'. The GTO, which stands for *Gran Turismo Omologato,* is powered by a 2,855cc 32-valve V8 engine with twin turbochargers and developing a massive 400bhp at a typically Ferrari engine speed of 7,000rpm. The turbo system and its ancillaries use much of the technology developed on Ferrari's turbocharged Grand Prix cars. For instance, Weber-Marelli IAW electronic injection and ignition are used, with each bank of cylinders having its own separate system. The transmission is entirely designed and made by Ferrari, and the single composite unit comprises the five-speed gearbox, clutch and limited-slip differential.

Four-wheel ventilated disc brakes are fitted but ABS is not deemed necessary. Suspension follows the Grand Prix car

The Ferrari GTO, introduced in mid-1984, amply underlines Ferrari's continued commitment to ultimate performance—having finally overtaken the legendary front-engined V12 Daytona as the fastest ever Ferrari road car.

layout, being independent all round and with coil springs and Koni dampers providing the springing medium. Slightly different wheel sizes are employed at front and rear, being 16 × 8in front and 16 × 10in at the rear, while Goodyear NCT tyres are supplied as standard fittings.

The body styling is very similar, but not identical, to the 308GTB Ferrari, and extensive use was made of wind tunnel testing to achieve a very aerodynamic shape. To meet racing homologation requirements, as its name implies, only 200 GTOs will be made and prices will be very high, at over £75,000 in Britain for example.

On the performance front, the 'off-the-shelf' GTO is reckoned to be good for 189mph and acceleration is equally stunning, with 0–62mph possible in under 5 seconds. As it is obvious that the standard 400bhp can easily be uprated to as much as 600bhp, even more shattering performance can be anticipated from the competition versions which are this car's *raison d'etre*.

S P E C I F I C A T I O N	
MODEL/TYPE	FERRARI GTO
ENGINE	V8, 2,855CC, TURBO
HORSEPOWER	400BHP @ 7,000RPM
TRANSMISSION	5-SPEED MANUAL
CHASSIS	STEEL TUBULAR
BRAKES	4-WHEEL DISC
TOP SPEED	190MPH PLUS
ACCELERATION 0–60MPH	4.9 SECS
PRODUCTION SPAN	1985 →

FERRARI TESTAROSSA

The next Ferrari carries the name of one of the most beautiful competition cars ever to race, the Testarossa, or Red Head. This name was given to the car because its cam covers were painted red instead of the more usual black. In the year of the original car's introduction, 1958, it won the 1,000km of Buenos Aires, the Sebring 12 hours, the Targa Florio and Le Mans. During the next year, success followed success for this lovely looking machine and so it is no surprise that Ferrari have seen fit to restore the name to their latest high performance car in 1985. The power comes from a 4,942cc flat-12, four-valve-per-cylinder engine mounted amidships in the car, and on top of the transmission. This impressive powerhouse produces 390bhp at 6,300rpm, to give the 1985 Testarossa a top speed of 181mph and acceleration from 0 to 62mph in 5.8 seconds.

The stunning body, like its predecessor, is from the studios of Pininfarina and, also like the earlier car, is like nothing else around today. The new radiator position, in the middle of the car instead of in the more usual place at the front, has been accommodated successfully in the body styling and although the car has its critics, to my mind Pininfarina have done an excellent job. The car is also very aerodynamically stable at all speeds, continuing the outstanding abilities of all recent Ferrari GT models.

The Testarossa's interior continues the constant improvement in driver and passenger accommodation that Ferraris have shown in the last few years and at the speeds that this car is capable of only the best ergonomics could be deemed as right. Noted journalist and former Ferrari team driver, Paul Frére, testing the new Testarossa, commented on the excellent roadholding and ride, the steering and braking performance, but added that the Ferrari trait of placing more emphasis on the engine than the chassis still remains in this latest Ferrari. Much as things change, they still remain the same, especially at Maranello!

By Ferrari standards, the styling of the new Testarossa is wildly extravagant but, as ever, the real story lies under the skin—in this case centering on the 5-litre 'boxer' engine with its red crackle-finish cam covers that give the car its name, Red Head.

S P E C I F I C A T I O N	
MODEL/TYPE	FERRARI TESTAROSSA
ENGINE	FLAT 12-CYL, DOHC
HORSEPOWER	390BHP @ 6,300RPM
TRANSMISSION	5-SPEED MANUAL
CHASSIS	TUBULAR STEEL
BRAKES	4-WHEEL DISC
TOP SPEED	181MPH
ACCELERATION 0–62MPH	5.8 SECS
PRODUCTION SPAN	1985 →

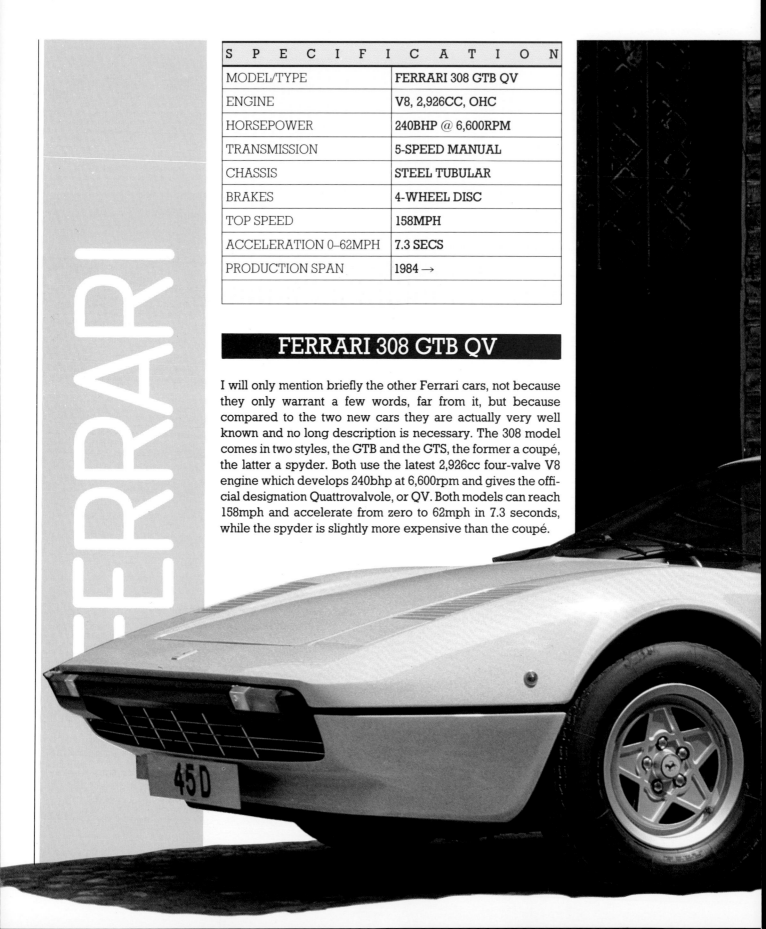

S P E C I F I C A T I O N	
MODEL/TYPE	FERRARI 308 GTB QV
ENGINE	V8, 2,926CC, OHC
HORSEPOWER	240BHP @ 6,600RPM
TRANSMISSION	5-SPEED MANUAL
CHASSIS	STEEL TUBULAR
BRAKES	4-WHEEL DISC
TOP SPEED	158MPH
ACCELERATION 0–62MPH	7.3 SECS
PRODUCTION SPAN	1984 →

FERRARI 308 GTB QV

I will only mention briefly the other Ferrari cars, not because they only warrant a few words, far from it, but because compared to the two new cars they are actually very well known and no long description is necessary. The 308 model comes in two styles, the GTB and the GTS, the former a coupé, the latter a spyder. Both use the latest 2,926cc four-valve V8 engine which develops 240bhp at 6,600rpm and gives the official designation Quattrovalvole, or QV. Both models can reach 158mph and accelerate from zero to 62mph in 7.3 seconds, while the spyder is slightly more expensive than the coupé.

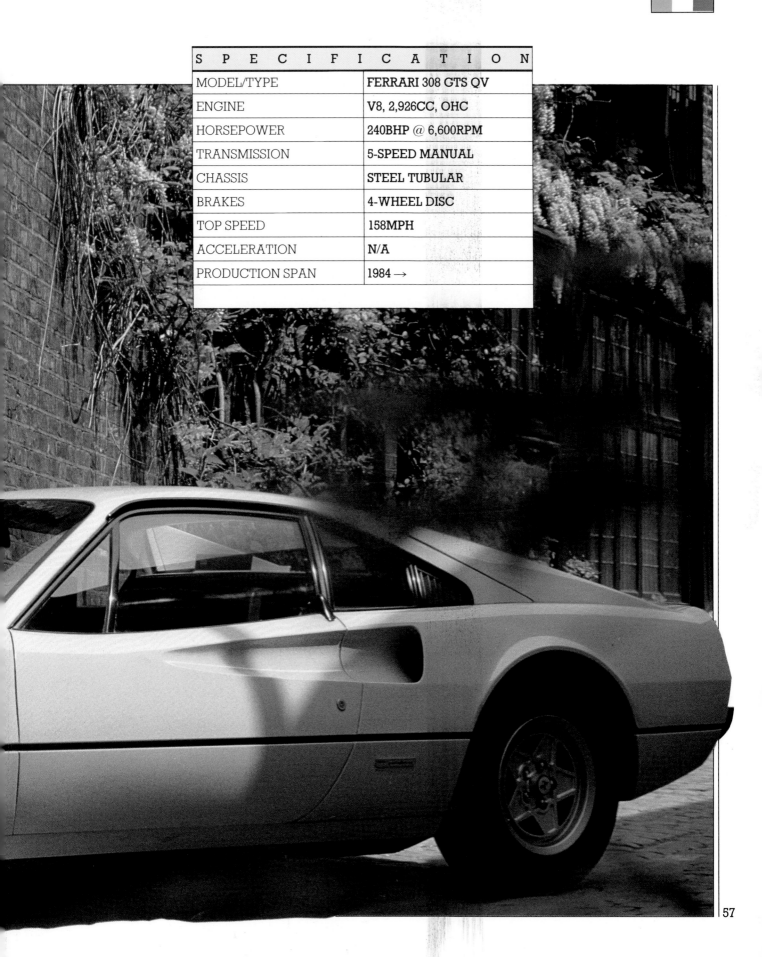

S P E C I F I C A T I O N	
MODEL/TYPE	FERRARI 308 GTS QV
ENGINE	V8, 2,926CC, OHC
HORSEPOWER	240BHP @ 6,600RPM
TRANSMISSION	5-SPEED MANUAL
CHASSIS	STEEL TUBULAR
BRAKES	4-WHEEL DISC
TOP SPEED	158MPH
ACCELERATION	N/A
PRODUCTION SPAN	1984 →

FERRARI

S P E C I F I C A T I O N	
MODEL/TYPE	FERRARI MONDIAL QV
ENGINE	V8, 2,926CC, SOHC
HORSEPOWER	240BHP @ 6,600RPM
TRANSMISSION	5-SPEED MANUAL
CHASSIS	STEEL MONOCOQUE
BRAKES	4-WHEEL DISC
TOP SPEED	149MPH
ACCELERATION 0–60MPH	6.4 SECS
PRODUCTION SPAN	1982 →

FERRARI MONDIAL QV

The Mondial model also comes in two similar body styles, and carries the same engine as the 308. Its top speed is 149mph and it will accelerate from 0–60mph in 6.4 seconds. As with the 308 spyder, the open-topped Mondial Cabriolet is rather more expensive than the coupé.

FERRARI 400i

The last Ferrari which I would mention is the 400i model, a full four-seater two-door car that is powered by a 4,823cc fuel-injected V12 engine. This car has the usual classic, ageless Pininfarina styling and despite being in production for many years still looks as up to date as any other performance car. It is one of the great classic cars of the modern era.

S P E C I F I C A T I O N	
MODEL/TYPE	FERRARI 400i
ENGINE	V12, 4,823CC, SOHC
HORSEPOWER	315BHP @ 6,400RPM
TRANSMISSION	5-SP/3-SP AUTO
CHASSIS	STEEL MONOCOQUE
BRAKES	4-WHEEL DISC
TOP SPEED	152MPH
ACCELERATION	N/A
PRODUCTION SPAN	1982 →

The supremely elegant 400i *(top right)* offers 150mph-plus Ferrari motoring for four and was the first Ferrari ever to offer automatic transmission. The Mondial Cabriolet *(opposite)* provides wind-in-the-hair motoring for a privileged few and its cockpit *(above)* combines leather-trimmed luxury with straightforward, strictly functional controls. The hardtop version of the Mondial is shown on pages 50–51.

The Ferrari 308GTB, styled by Pininfarina, was originally introduced in 1975 with a glass reinforced plastic body, but within a couple of years it reverted to a metal shell, under which now lurks a 240bhp four-valve V8 which is unmistakably Ferrari *(previous page)*.

MASERATI

Like Lancia and Alfa Romeo, Maserati have had a long and often financially difficult history in fast car production. The company was founded by the five Maserati brothers, Carlo, Bindo, Alfieri, Mario and Ernesto in 1926 and their early cars were tough, hand-built, sensible machines for the competition driver. Always short of money really to develop their ideas, the brothers soldiered on until they were forced to sell out to the Orsi industrial combine in 1938, with Omer Orsi taking over as managing director. The company is now owned by the Argentine Alessandro De Tomaso who has continued the policy of building high quality, durable cars of high performance. One of the nicest touches about Maserati, even after several changes of ownership, is that the factory address still commemorates one of the brothers, Alfieri — the engineering genius of the family.

I would like to mention just two of their cars, the Merak SS and the Khamsin, as I feel that these are the two that embody all the finest qualities of the Maserati marque.

MASERATI MERAK SS

The Merak was first shown at the 1975 Geneva Auto Show. As with all Giugiaro-styled cars, it is very good looking, from every angle. Fit and finish of the bodywork are good rather than excellent and like all Italian cars, whatever their cost, any lapse in maintenance, cosmetic or mechanical, very soon shows itself. Some neglected five-year-old Meraks look ten times their age, while equally old models that have received regular loving attention look almost new.

Any mid-engined 2+2 car loses out in two major respects over more conventional, front-engined models, in accessibility to the engine and in a definite lack of real luggage carrying capacity. In these failings, however, the Merak is no better or worse than any similar car, and in one other respect the Merak is outstandingly good for a mid-engined car; unlike most, its three-quarter rear view vision is good, as the usual blind spot is much reduced by the use of the flying buttress rear window arrangement devised by Giugiaro.

The Merak SS's engine is a 2,965cc V6 with double overhead camshafts driven by a duplex chain. This engine produces 208bhp at 5,800rpm on three Weber twin-choke carburettors — two are 42DCNF31s and the third is a single 42DCNF32. This is enough to carry the car to a top speed of 143mph. However, there is one drawback to this engine, on driving the Merak at maximum revs for any length of time an alarming drop in registered oil pressure is noticed. This may be due to the all-alloy engine flexing, allowing the main bearings to release pressure, with dire effects on engine life. The maker's handbook simply recommends that the engine shouldn't be run at maximum speed for extended periods but there is no rev-limiting device to guard against this problem.

The lack of a modern fuel-injection system shows up in temperamental cold starts and fussy driving habits until the engine is fully warmed up. Fuel consumption averages out at about 18mpg, so that even with the 18.7-gallon tank only about 350 miles are possible between refills.

On the road, the Merak behaves like any good mid-engined car. It is stable, with a reasonable amount of understeer at all times, its ride is choppy at low speeds, improving with an increase in speed to become acceptable. Braking is by the Citroën high-pressure system and really isn't well suited to such a high performance machine, as its over-sensitivity hardly makes for smooth, fast progress.

The driving compartment is comfortable, with enough room for two average-sized adults, but the heating and ventilation systems are no better than poor, taking a very long time to warm up and then control of the heat is difficult and the ventilation almost non-existent! Air-conditioning is available as an extra, and is almost a necessity. The Merak is not a cheap car and is really for Maserati-lovers only, as there are certainly better value cars of similar performance on the market.

Somehow, the Maserati name has never had quite the same *cachet* as Ferrari, but the Neptune's trident badge of the city of Bologna has nonetheless graced some superb cars.
The Maserati Merak SS *(opposite and previous page)* was introduced in 1975, the year in which Citroën, who had rescued the Bolognese company in 1968, relinquished control to Allesandro de Tomaso. Under de Tomaso's management, Maserati has made a remarkable recovery and for once in its troubled history can face the future with real confidence.

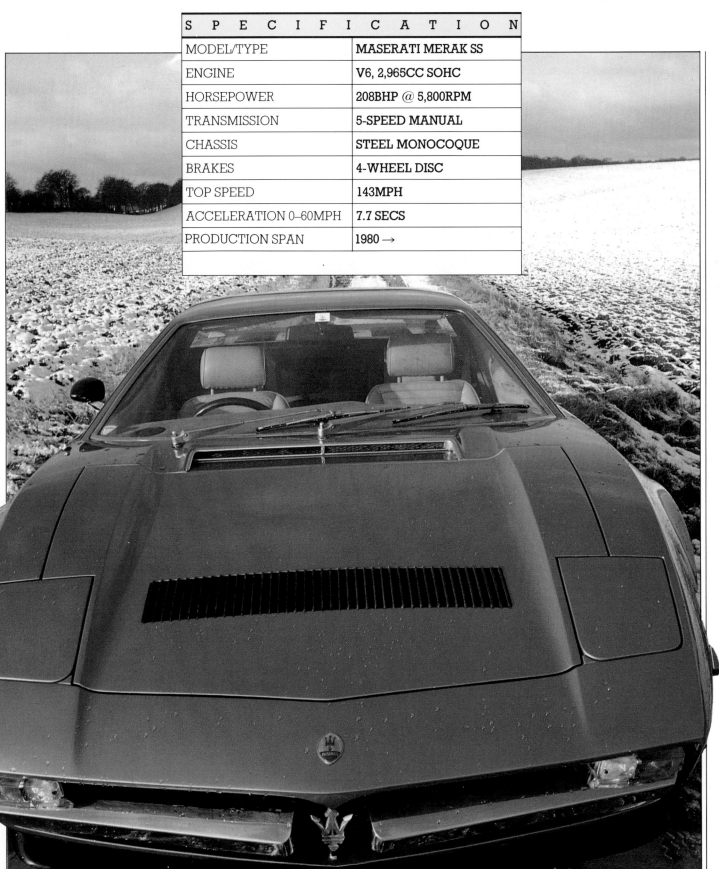

S P E C I F I C A T I O N	
MODEL/TYPE	MASERATI MERAK SS
ENGINE	V6, 2,965CC SOHC
HORSEPOWER	208BHP @ 5,800RPM
TRANSMISSION	5-SPEED MANUAL
CHASSIS	STEEL MONOCOQUE
BRAKES	4-WHEEL DISC
TOP SPEED	143MPH
ACCELERATION 0–60MPH	7.7 SECS
PRODUCTION SPAN	1980 →

MASERATI KHAMSIN

The Khamsin model is the final embodiment of the great front-engined, high-speed Maseratis, like the Mexico and the Mistral. As a design, it is now nearly 12 years old and many aspects of the car show this fact very clearly. The handsome body houses a front-mounted 4,700cc V8 engine, with double overhead cams, driven by a duplex chain. This power unit breathes through four Weber 42DCNF41 carburettors and produces 280bhp at 5,500rpm.

The Khamsin body although officially described as a 2+2 is really only a two-seater, as rear leg and head room are minimal at best. Accommodation for two, however, is comfortable, although the seats are covered in rather slippery leather, which, together with a strange lack of lateral support makes for less than positive driver location. The steering and seats are adjusted hydraulically, and the steering column can be adjusted for both length and rake by this system. The body styling is tasteful and the car is very well finished. The Khamsin is also very reasonably priced for a car that will reach 160mph and accelerate from 0 to 60mph in 6.5 seconds.

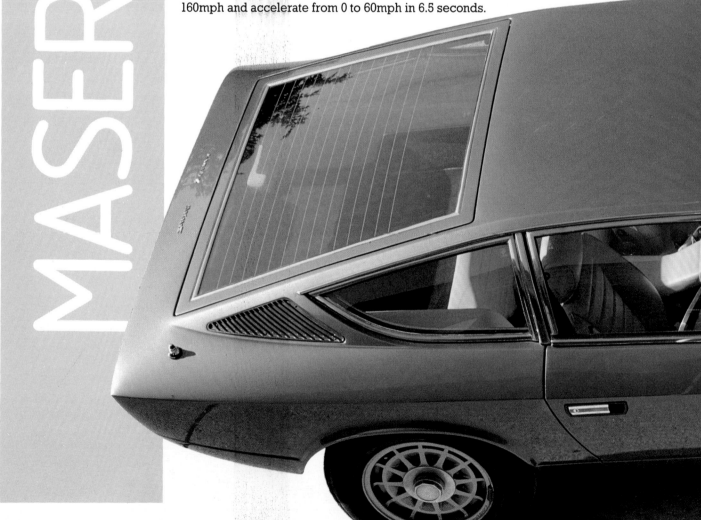

MASERATI

S P E C I F I C A T I O N	
MODEL/TYPE	MASERATI KHAMSIN
ENGINE	V8, 4,700CC DOHC
HORSEPOWER	280BHP @ 5,500RPM
TRANSMISSION	5-SPEED MANUAL
CHASSIS	STEEL MONOCOQUE
BRAKES	4-WHEEL DISC
TOP SPEED	160MPH
ACCELERATION 0–60MPH	6.5 SECS
PRODUCTION SPAN	1978 →

Although the Bertone-styled Maserati Khamsin, introduced in 1974, is now growing somewhat long in the tooth, it must still be regarded as a classic example of the traditional big front-engined supercar.

LAMBORGHINI COUNTACH S

LAMBORGHINI

Lamborghini is the relative newcomer among the classic Italian makes, but its engineering is second to none and its Countach S is arguably the most dramatic of all fast cars. It has one of the most outrageously extrovert bodies any car has ever been given. Standing still, it really does *look* as if it is doing 200mph! Although it is by no means a practical car, the Countach S makes the biggest automotive statement of any car on the road today. One problem for any owner of a Countach S, however, is that he must expect to be stopped fairly regularly by the police just because the car looks too fast for its own good!

What's more, it *is* fast; very fast. The 4,754cc double overhead cam V12 engine is rated at 375bhp at 7,000rpm. This gives the car a top speed of 174mph, accelerating it to 100mph from rest in 12.9 seconds! The car's performance really does match its appearance. It can stop too, with massive disc brakes all round, which will deliver 1.1g deceleration, stopping the car from 30mph in under 28 feet. Fuel consumption is only an average of 16mpg but with all this performance on hand who worries about the fuel bills?

If you've got it, flaunt it! The dramatic Lamborghini Countach S most certainly has it and isn't exactly shy about admitting it . . .

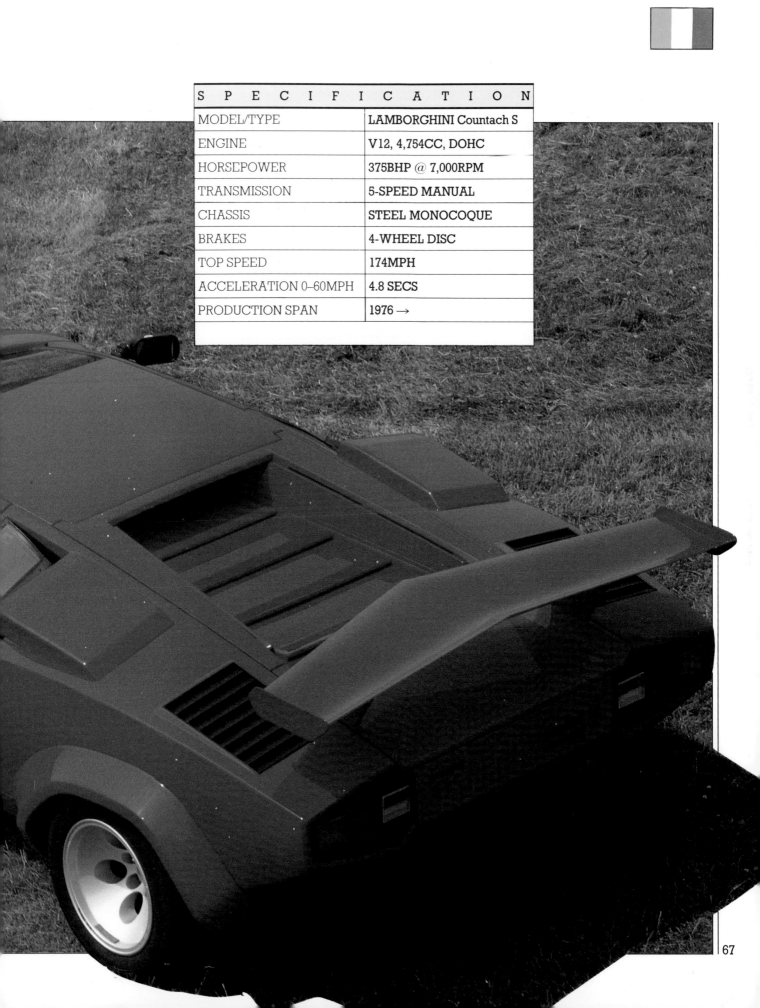

SPECIFICATION	
MODEL/TYPE	LAMBORGHINI Countach S
ENGINE	V12, 4,754CC, DOHC
HORSEPOWER	375BHP @ 7,000RPM
TRANSMISSION	5-SPEED MANUAL
CHASSIS	STEEL MONOCOQUE
BRAKES	4-WHEEL DISC
TOP SPEED	174MPH
ACCELERATION 0–60MPH	4.8 SECS
PRODUCTION SPAN	1976 →

FIAT

My last selection for these ranks of fast Italian cars comes from Fiat, and it is the unexpectedly rapid Uno Turbo model. This car, which was launched in Rio during the weekend of the Brazilian Grand Prix in April 1985, has a turbocharged 1.3-litre engine with water injection and 105bhp, which gives the little hatchback a claimed top speed of 125mph and a zero to 62mph time of 8.3 seconds. It can also claim an overall fuel consumption of some 32mpg!

No price has been decided on but sales will begin late in 1985 and the Uno Turbo should be a welcome addition to the growing ranks of small, really fast cars.

With the exception of this forthcoming Fiat, really fast Italian cars are invariably exotic and very expensive, but for his money the buyer gets not only high performance but that other sought-after quality, exclusivity. There are some places in the world where Porsches seem as common as Volkswagen Beetles — just take a look at southern California for instance. Even in California though, the sight of a Ferrari Testarossa or a Lamborghini Countach S is a very rare treat.

Despite the imposition of speed limits (which few Italian drivers observe) Italy still makes very fast cars and makes them better than ever before; long may it continue to do so.

The boxy Fiat Uno Turbo may look like a fish out of water in this hallowed company of supercars but the mixture of small hatchback and turbo power adds up to a few surprises for 'real' sportscar drivers.

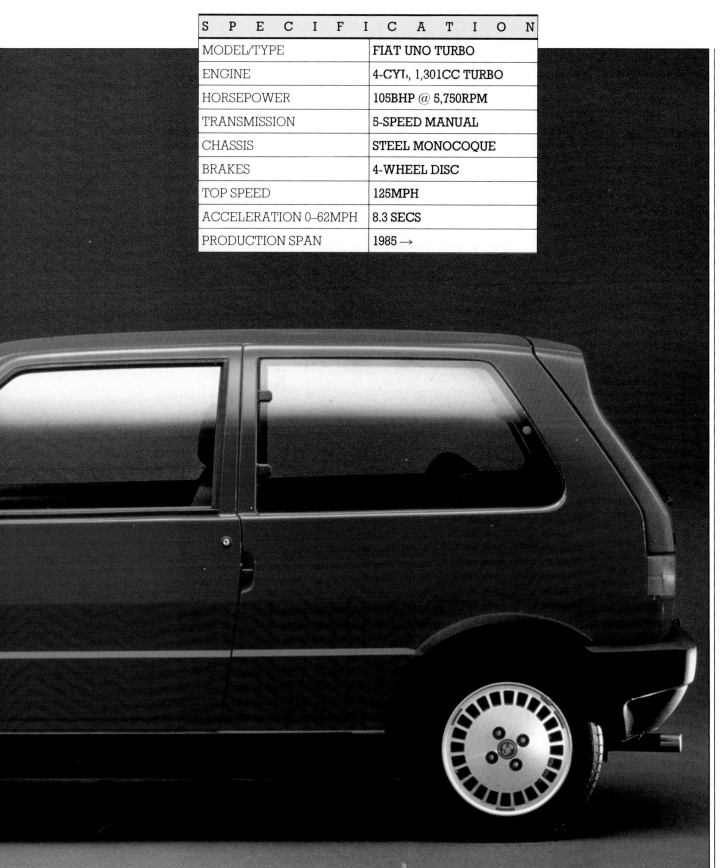

S P E C I F I C A T I O N	
MODEL/TYPE	FIAT UNO TURBO
ENGINE	4-CYL, 1,301CC TURBO
HORSEPOWER	105BHP @ 5,750RPM
TRANSMISSION	5-SPEED MANUAL
CHASSIS	STEEL MONOCOQUE
BRAKES	4-WHEEL DISC
TOP SPEED	125MPH
ACCELERATION 0–62MPH	8.3 SECS
PRODUCTION SPAN	1985 →

GREAT BRITAIN

Great Britain has always had its share of the fast car market, from Napiers before World War I, Bentleys after it, and Jaguars, Aston Martins, Bristols and AC Cobras since. Unlike those of many other countries, the British fast car industry has been heavily handicapped by speed limits, high insurance premiums and by the lack of a really rich mass of population wanting, and able to buy, expensive fast cars. However, in today's world and in spite of speed limits, there are more fast cars available to the British consumer than at any time in the country's motoring history. They range from the very expensive to the affordable. I will comment on thirteen (out of a list of several more) in this chapter.

Tackling them in alphabetical order, I will start with two Aston Martin models, the Lagonda and the Vantage. Both are very expensive, as befits hand-made vehicles. The Lagonda is priced at £65,999 on its home market, or almost twice the price of a Porsche 928. The Vantage costs £52,494, and both cars, even at these prices, are in considerable demand by customers all over the world. They combine the twin advantages of being rare items to be seen on the road and of having very high performance.

The best of British? Wind in the hair performance or exclusive elegance are both available from Aston Martin with the Vantage (*left*) or the strikingly individual and very rare Lagonda (*below*).

ASTON MARTIN LAGONDA

The Lagonda has a 5,340cc double overhead cam V8 engine breathing through four Weber 42DCNF90/100 carburettors. The Aston Martin factory in the small town of Newport Pagnell does not quote horsepower figures but the German ministry of transport requires all cars sold in the Federal Republic to disclose their power outputs and for that requirement Aston Martin have quoted a figure of 390bhp, which must be close to the mark.

Transmission from the front-mounted engine is via a Chrysler Torqueflite automatic gearbox to a chassis-mounted limited-slip differential. Front suspension is by the classic unequal length wishbone, coil-spring and damper set up, with an anti-roll bar. The rear suspension is self-levelling and features a de Dion axle. Steering is by power-assisted rack and pinion and brakes are ventilated disc units all round. The Lagonda uses 15 × 6in alloy wheels fitted as standard with the superb Avon Turbospeed 235/70 VR 15 tyres.

The car's instruments use digital LED displays and cover all possible information that the driver may need. The Lagonda weighs 4,622lb, has a top speed of 143mph and takes just 20.8 seconds to reach 100mph from a standstill. The William Towns-designed body is striking in appearance and certainly has looks in keeping with the price. The whole car exudes luxury and high performance

This classic power unit was introduced in 1970 and by 1972 it had replaced the long-serving six-cylinder unit as the standard Aston Martin engine. Most specialist manufacturers looking for more horsepower tend to turn to big, easily available American V8s but it is typical of Aston Martin's integrity that they looked to their own drawing boards and came up with an engine which powers not only their road cars but also the company's Nimrod Group C racing sportscar.

S P E C I F I C A T I O N	
MODEL/TYPE	ASTON MARTIN Lagonda
ENGINE	V8, 5,340CC, SOHC
HORSEPOWER	N/A
TRANSMISSION	3-SPEED AUTO
CHASSIS	STEEL
BRAKES	4-WHEEL DISC
TOP SPEED	143MPH
ACCELERATION 0–60MPH	8.9 SECS
PRODUCTION SPAN	1980 →

Tickford is Aston Martin Lagonda's advanced engineering and styling arm and even the lines of the stunning Lagonda saloon, originally styled by Bill Towns, can benefit from the Tickford touch.

ASTON MARTIN VANTAGE

The Aston Martin Vantage is a sports coupé in the old style, big, very fast, very expensive, constructed in the finest materials, and very beautifully finished. The car uses the same hand-built V8 engine as the Lagonda but with high-performance camshafts and bigger Weber 48IDF 3/150 carburettors increasing both power and torque. The gearbox is the ZF five-speed manual model which is heavy in operation but otherwise superb. Wheel sizes are also uprated compared to the Lagonda, to 15 × 8in and standard tyres are 275/55 VR 15 Pirelli P7s.

The Vantage is shatteringly fast, with a 168mph top speed and acceleration from 0 to 100mph in 11.9 seconds. Don't ask about fuel consumption which averages only 9–10mpg; in this league, such calculations never come into the equation. For such a large car, the Vantage is, surprisingly, really only a two-seater. Space for passengers in the back is, at best, minimal. Agility on twisty roads is obviously limited by sheer size, the car being much more suitable for long high-speed journeys preferably by unrestricted motorway.

The Aston Martin Vantage is the ultimate example of the traditional British sports coupé and if it is ever dropped from production by the powers-that-be at Newport Pagnell it will be sorely missed, even by those who will never be able to afford to buy one.

The Aston Martin Vantage (*inset*) and the drophead Volante (*below*) both look, and indeed feel, big, but their lusty V8 engines — all built by hand and each bearing its builder's name on a brass plate — make them two of the fastest cars in the world.

S P E C I F I C A T I O N	
MODEL/TYPE	**ASTON MARTIN** Vantage
ENGINE	V8, 5,340CC, SOHC
HORSEPOWER	N/A
TRANSMISSION	5-SPEED MANUAL
CHASSIS	STEEL
BRAKES	4-WHEEL DISC
TOP SPEED	168MPH
ACCELERATION 0–60MPH	5.2 SECS
PRODUCTION SPAN	1978 →

Next on the list are three cars from the Bristol Car Company, the Britannia, the Beaufighter and the Brigand—all named after famous Bristol aircraft from the company's earlier days. Although Bristol now use American V8 engines, the big, luxuriously appointed and extremely quick cars are in reality archetypally British. They are thoroughly conventional, even a little old fashioned in overall concept, but what they lack in high technology or advanced thinking they more than make up for in engineering quality.

This is a logical result of a background in aero engineering, where fundamental change is slow but quality is everything. Aircraft were Bristol's forté up to the end of the war in 1945, when the Bristol Aircraft Company sought new employment for suddenly redundant production capacity and opened a car division—which had been under consideration even during the war.

The first Bristol car, launched in 1947, was based on much-improved prewar BMW six-cylinder engines and chassis, rights to which Bristol had acquired as wartime reparations. Bristol's main improvements to the BMW engines were in the use of superior materials—unavailable in prewar Germany as high-grade metals were already being diverted to military use.

With these first cars, the Bristol reputation for performance with quality was born. The Bristol has never been a slavish follower of fashion, never for instance changing its shape simply to attract a fickle buying public. The cars are made by hand, slowly and at a rate of only three a week. They are bought and driven, usually with some verve, by real enthusiasts. Packard used to use the slogan 'Ask the man who owns one' and every Packard owner by implication became an unpaid salesman. Bristol might use the same words; every single Bristol owner I have ever met loves his car (or sometimes cars) and cannot wait to start selling the virtues of the make to anyone who will listen.

From the BMW-engined models, Bristol developed their own, classic, hemi-headed straight-six engine and this, in superbly developed chassis, was used until 1961. Then, having rejected the option of building their own V8 engine as being too expensive for three cars a week, Bristol began its association with American power which continues in the superb cars described here.

BRISTOL BRIGAND

The most expensive of the current Bristol range is the Brigand, a turbocharged two-door four-seater saloon whose sleek lines date back to 1978 and the introduction of what was then known as the 603 saloon. At a price in Britain of £52,692, the Brigand costs a few pounds more than the thoroughbred Aston Martin Vantage and not much less than the normally-aspirated version of the Bentley Mulsanne—each of which uses its own

design and make of V8. This is not to imply that the Bristol is in any way inferior, in fact at least one magazine road-tester has described the Bristol as being, overall, the best car in the world, at any price.

That, as with any car, is open to endless argument, but with a top speed of 150mph and the ability to reach 60mph from rest in under six seconds, the Brigand is not as quick as the Vantage (but then nor is much else) but will comfortably outrun the 'ordinary' Mulsanne.

Part of the Bristol's strength lies in its chassis performance, where the engineering quality is really evident, and although it will give best place to many modern supercars, its ride and handling are quite exceptional for such a luxurious, spacious saloon.

S P E C I F I C A T I O N	
MODEL/TYPE	BRISTOL BRIGAND
ENGINE	CHRYSLER V8, TURBO
HORSEPOWER	N/A
TRANSMISSION	CHRYSLER AUTO
CHASSIS	BOX SECTION STEEL
BRAKES	4-WHEEL DISC
TOP SPEED	150MPH
ACCELERATION 0–60MPH	5.9 SECS
PRODUCTION SPAN	1984 →

Although many other Anglo-American hybrids have been hastily conceived and appropriately short-lived, the 140mph Bristol Britannia saloon shows that a marriage of the best British engineering and an American mass-produced power unit can result in a genuine classic car.

BRISTOL

100 MPH

S P E C I F I C A T I O N	
MODEL/TYPE	**BRISTOL BEAUFIGHTER**
ENGINE	**CHRYSLER V8, TURBO**
HORSEPOWER	**N/A**
TRANSMISSION	**CHRYSLER AUTO**
CHASSIS	**STEEL BOX SECTION**
BRAKES	**4-WHEEL DISC**
TOP SPEED	**150MPH**
ACCELERATION 0–60MPH	**5.9 SECS**
PRODUCTION SPAN	**1984 →**

BRISTOL BEAUFIGHTER

The most glamorous of the Bristol range, if such a term is appropriate, is the turbocharged Beaufighter, which shares the same version of the Chrysler hemi as the Brigand saloon. The Beaufighter however is a much more distinctive and rather angular car, distinguished by its flamboyant targa-type top, with a substantial roll-hoop and a lift off centre section.

The car was styled by Zagato and introduced as the 412 Convertible, later known as the Convertible Saloon, in 1975. Also among its styling features is the traditional Bristol way of housing the spare wheel in a concealed compartment in the front wing. The turbocharged version and the Beaufighter name were launched in 1980 and the superb car has been little changed since then.

Like the similarly-powered Brigand, it will reach 150mph and cover zero to 60mph in 5.9 seconds. The Beaufighter is the cheapest car in the Bristol range but with only a little change from £50,000 on the British market it is marginally more expensive than the cheapest Aston Martin or the newly introduced Bentley Eight—its most obvious esoteric British rivals. Price however is not the most important consideration at this end of the market and the Bristol appeal is unique. For such large, heavy and well-equipped machines they are surprisingly light in feel, easy to drive well and only a little harder to drive really quickly. What more could any sybaritic enthusiast ask?

BENTLEY MULSANNE

When the Bentley company was sold to Rolls-Royce in 1931 it was soon apparent that the old Bentley, the blood-and-guts fast sportscar, would be smoothed and softened into no more than a very nice but unremarkable open Rolls-Royce, and the days of real performance would be over. It took Rolls-Royce 51 years to introduce a Bentley that was more than a re-badged, re-radiatored Rolls-Royce. The Mulsanne model, named after the famous straight on the Le Mans racing circuit, the scene of the beginning of the old Bentley legend, is, at last, a really fast Bentley, one that W. O. Bentley himself would certainly not have disowned. W.O. always disliked and would have nothing to do with supercharged engines, feeling that if more power was required he could easily provide it with more capacity, while retaining all the flexibility and reliability that his cars were renowned for. In his day the supercharger was not for the ordinary motorist and was justifiably viewed with suspicion when fitted to an everyday car.

The Mulsanne has changed all that, for it is one of the very best of the current crop of boosted induction cars. Its 6.75-litre V8 engine produces an undisclosed amount of power, but sufficient to propel the heavy car (weighing 5,051lb) to speeds of over 130mph and from zero to 60mph in 7.4 seconds. It seats four people in great comfort and can transport them with a smoothness and speed that are uncanny. Handling is a little 'soft', with rather too much roll in cornering but a Bentley is not usually hustled around like a Ferrari and with normal Bentley-style driving it is a delight — albeit an expensive delight at £63,288 on its home market. Rolls-Royce-made automobiles have a justified reputation for retaining their resale value better than most other cars and it is almost certain that the Mulsanne will be one of the great collectors' cars of the not-too-distant future, fetching very high prices.

S P E C I F I C A T I O N	
MODEL/TYPE	BENTLEY MULSANNE
ENGINE	V8, 6,750CC, TURBO
HORSEPOWER	N/A
TRANSMISSION	3-SPEED AUTO
CHASSIS	STEEL MONOCOQUE
BRAKES	4-WHEEL DISC
TOP SPEED	135MPH
ACCELERATION 0–60MPH	7.4 SECS
PRODUCTION SPAN	1984 →

BENTLEY

Ettore Bugatti once described the Bentleys which beat his own cars at Le Mans in the 1920s as *'les plus vites camions du monde'*—the fastest lorries in the world. No lorry however was ever as fast or as luxurious as the Bentley Mulsanne, named for the famous straight on the Le Mans circuit where Bentleys had their finest hour.

FORD

At the other end of the price and exclusivity spectrum are Ford's two fast cars in Great Britain, the XR4i and the Capri Special Injection. These two follow in the tradition of all Ford products in offering fine value-for-money vehicles, and in both cases they also have the bonus of being very fast!

FORD CAPRI 2.8i

The Capri was originally introduced in 1968 and like the Porsche 911 has so far refused to lie down and die, but now it looks as if 1985 will be positively the last year for the Capri as we know it and a replacement is already being developed to go into the dealers in the spring of 1986.

It is not difficult to understand why the Capri has lasted so long. It is a good looking car and it performs well — especially in the old 3-litre version and in the current 2.8-litre model. It is backed by one of the biggest service organizations in the world and parts and maintenance for it are not expensive. In short, it works and the customers love it!

The present ultimate Capri in Europe is the Injection Special, and for just under £10,000 in Britain the customer will get a stylish, hatchback coupé, that is well made and well finished, that will deliver 160bhp from its Bosch K-Jetronic injected engine, enough to hit 125mph in fourth gear at 5,700rpm. Acceleration from 0 to 60mph is also very brisk at 7.9 seconds.

Apart from sheer performance, what does the Injection Special offer the buyer over and above the 'ordinary' Capri? Well, for the extra money, the buyer gets Recaro seating, a leather-bound steering wheel, alloy road wheels and a limited slip differential. Fuel economy, which is most important in any Ford model, works out at an average of 25mpg, and that is very good in view of the car's performance.

Riding on 205/60 VR 13 Goodyear NCT tyres, the Capri is a marvellous car to drive fast on dry roads and its basic over-steer characteristics allow the competent driver to explore really fast cornering in great safety. In the wet, however, it is a different story and care has to be exercised, because as with any front-engined, nose-heavy car, the tail can move out too far if the driver is careless. Braking is initially good but from really high speeds there is a lack of real bite and stopping from speed can be ragged. Nevertheless, the Capri remains one of the best performance-for-money buys around today and Ford will have a very hard job replacing it

Both top-of-the-range cars use essentially the same V6 engine (with minor power output differences) and the same five-speed gearbox, but the utterly conventional Capri is still the cheaper of the two—and the better equipped. Although four-wheel-drive and turbocharged Sierras are also now available, it will probably be a long time before the new car's popularity reaches the peaks once enjoyed by the Capri.

S P E C I F I C A T I O N	
MODEL/TYPE	FORD CAPRI 2.8i
ENGINE	V6, 2,792CC
HORSEPOWER	160BHP @ 5,700RPM
TRANSMISSION	5-SPEED MANUAL
CHASSIS	STEEL MONOCOQUE
BRAKES	4-WHEEL DISC
TOP SPEED	130MPH
ACCELERATION 0–60MPH	7.9 SECS
PRODUCTION SPAN	1968 →

Power to the people! Ford may not build a true sportscar but the 2.8 injection version of the enormously popular Capri coupé offers exciting performance without breaking the bank—although not for much longer.

FORD

S P E C I F I C A T I O N	
MODEL/TYPE	FORD SIERRA XR4i
ENGINE	V6, 2,792CC
HORSEPOWER	150BHP @ 5,700RPM
TRANSMISSION	5-SPEED MANUAL
CHASSIS	STEEL MONOCOQUE
BRAKES	4-WHEEL DISC
TOP SPEED	130MPH
ACCELERATION 0–60MPH	8 SECS
PRODUCTION SPAN	1982 →

FORD SIERRA XR4i

The Sierra XR4i can perhaps best be thought of as a four-seater version of what the new Capri will offer in coupé form. As with the Capri, a front-mounted pushrod V6 engine is used to drive the rear wheels via a five-speed manual gearbox. The 2,792cc engine develops 150bhp at 5,700rpm. The Sierra's suspension, unlike the Capri's, is all-independent, and its brakes are ventilated front discs and rear drums, these just like the Capri. Because of the XR4i's more aerodynamic shape, it slips through the air much better than the older Capri and the lower horsepower actually produces both better acceleration, with 0–60mph in 8.4 seconds, and a higher top speed, at 130mph. Over long distances the XR4i's quieter mode of travel is considerably less tiring than the Capri. Lacking a limited slip differential, however, and on narrower 195/60 VR 14 Goodyear NCT tyres, the XR4i is not so pleasant to drive fast as the Capri, it feels 'looser', and the power-assisted steering is not so crisp and accurate in feel as that of the Capri. The Sierra's braking has a better feel than the Capri's stoppers, but the brakes tend to be noisy when used hard.

The XR4i really takes off where the Capri finishes, it is a very good car, capable of much development over the next few years and it seems likely that it will simply get better and better as time passes.

There has also been some debate over the Sierra's high-speed stability in strong crosswinds and this has added—probably more than the car deserves—to the worrying sales resistance caused initially by the controversial styling. Ford are certainly keeping faith with the Sierra however, both in Europe and in America, where the car is the basis of the turbo-engined Merkur, described later.

The Ford Sierra's styling is nothing if not controversial; variously loved or hated, it has been affectionately dubbed 'the jelly mould'. With typically accurate feel for what the people want, Ford gave the XR4-i its bi-plane spoiler and racier trim and created a totally different image which spoke of performance.

FORD (SA) XR8

In July 1984 Ford of South Africa announced a variation on the XR4i theme, the XR8. This is a limited edition of the Sierra model but with the Mustang V8 engine, rated at 200bhp, plus a five-speed close-ratio gearbox and with disc brakes fitted all round. If the specification sounds rather on the racy side, then it will come as no surprise to learn that the XR8 is intended as an homologation special so that Ford of South Africa can go production saloon car racing. The 5-litre engine will run the car up to more than 140mph and from 0 to 62mph in less than 8 seconds. The car has the five-door body shell and it will be offered only in white. Only 250 examples will be built and all of them are expected to be sold before the last car is finished, at a price which has not yet been announced but is likely to be substantial.

S P E C I F I C A T I O N	
MODEL/TYPE	FORD (SA) XR8
ENGINE	V8, 5,000CC
HORSEPOWER	200BHP @ 4,800RPM
TRANSMISSION	5-SPEED MANUAL
CHASSIS	STEEL MONOCOQUE
BRAKES	4-WHEEL DISC
TOP SPEED	140MPH PLUS
ACCELERATION 0–60MPH	7.6 SECS
PRODUCTION SPAN	1984 →

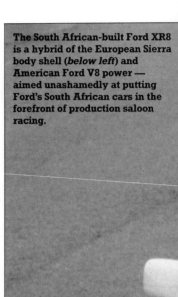

The South African-built Ford XR8 is a hybrid of the European Sierra body shell (*below left*) and American Ford V8 power — aimed unashamedly at putting Ford's South African cars in the forefront of production saloon racing.

FORD

Since the introduction of the XK-120, Jaguar have established themselves as the makers of some of the finest high speed cars in the world — at any price. Classic examples include the 150S, the C-type, D-type and E-type models, the fabulous, one-off XK-13, the XJ-S and the superb XJ-S HE. All but one of Jaguar's current cars will exceed 125mph and the XJ-S HE will reach 155mph!

JAGUAR XJ-6

I intend to look at two models, the XJ-S HE and the XJ-6 4.2-litre. The latter is powered by an in-line six-cylinder twin-cam engine, possibly the final flowering of the same engine that powered the XK-120 over 30 years ago. It now uses Bosch L-Jetronic fuel injection to produce 205bhp at 5,000rpm and this is enough to propel the car to a top speed of 130mph, and accelerate it from a standstill to 60mph in 9.8 seconds, in spite of a weight of 4,035lb.

As with all the XJ models, that is not the whole story. It is much more the manner of the Jaguar's performance that is important. On a value-for-money basis there is nothing to touch the way the Jaguar goes about its work. Smoothly, very quietly and with a silky quality that nothing else can match, the car from Brown's Lane, Coventry puts every other high-quality fast car into the shade.

Until the arrival of John Egan, as managing director, Jaguar suffered from a build quality problem, but under his direction this has changed dramatically; and there are even waiting lists. Buyers are snapping up all models of the car world-wide. This Jaguar revival is particularly apparent in North America and in Germany, where sales have taken off in the last two years to such an extent that in some places a premium has to be paid to get a new Jaguar!

S P E C I F I C A T I O N	
MODEL/TYPE	JAGUAR XJ-6
ENGINE	6-CYL, 4,235CC, DOHC
HORSEPOWER	205BHP @ 5,000RPM
TRANSMISSION	5-SP/3-SP AUTO
CHASSIS	STEEL MONOCOQUE
BRAKES	4-WHEEL DISC
TOP SPEED	130MPH
ACCELERATION 0–60MPH	9.8 SECS
PRODUCTION SPAN	1984 →

Unmistakably Jaguar: the simple lines of the XJ-6 are instantly recognizable as a product of Britain's best known maker of sportscars and luxury sporting saloons.

JAGUAR

JAGUAR XJ-S HE

If it is a two seater or 2+2 Jaguar that is required then the XJ-S HE model is the one to go for. Equipped with a fuel-injected V12 engine that even Mercedes-Benz admit is the best mass-produced high performance engine made anywhere in the world, the big coupé has no real rival at its home market price of £23,385. The 5.3-litre overhead-cam engine uses Bosch digital electronic fuel injection and an electronic ignition system. Fuel economy works out at 22.5mpg at 75mph, which is quite remarkable for this large, very fast car which will reach 155mph and storm from zero to 60mph in 7.5 seconds.

Both these cars are beautifully made and finished and Jaguar cannot build enough to meet the current demand for either of them.

Jaguar purists may never have been quite sure about the XJ-S's controversial shape but this car, with its superb V12 engine, is quite simply one of the best cars in the world at any price.

S P E C I F I C A T I O N	
MODEL/TYPE	JAGUAR XJ-S HE
ENGINE	V12, 5,345CC, DOHC
HORSEPOWER	299BHP @ 5,500RPM
TRANSMISSION	3-SPEED AUTO
CHASSIS	STEEL MONOCOQUE
BRAKES	4-WHEEL DISC
TOP SPEED	155MPH
ACCELERATION 0–60MPH	7.5 SECS
PRODUCTION SPAN	1980 →

LOTUS

As with Jaguar, I have selected two cars from the Lotus range, the Excel and the Esprit Turbo, to demonstrate the special Lotus qualities. For 1985 Lotus have revised these models quite significantly, with new body styling, wheels and tyres, electrics, instruments, air conditioning, hard trim and soft trim. The new body is certainly better looking than the old, it is cleaner and more 'of a piece' than before. The chassis is still the familiar steel backbone with a five-year anti-corrision warranty. Thanks to the restyled body, the rear window is 25% bigger and access to the boot is much improved. New VDO instruments called Night Design have been relocated in the dash panel to better effect.

The engine is the 912-type 2.2-litre 16-valve double overhead cam four-cylinder unit, which produces 160bhp at 6,500rpm. A five-speed gearbox is used and rear-wheel drive. All-independent suspension displays all the features that Lotus are famous for, the very highest levels of roadholding with no sacrifice to ride or comfort. Power-assistance to the rack-and-pinion steering is optional. Ventilated disc brakes are used all round and the system is servo-assisted. Alloy road wheels of 14 × 7in carry 205/60 VR 14 Goodyear NCT tyres.

LOTUS EXCEL

The Excel has the performance to go with its good looks, with a top speed of 134mph and 0–100mph in 20 seconds, with a fuel consumption of 29.4mpg at 75mph. A colleague who loves Porsches recently reported that he had tried a new Excel and was astonished not only at how well it performed but also at the very high standards of build quality. There is no denying that for far too long Lotus have had a very poor reputation for quality in their cars but in the last two or three years they have made great efforts to overcome these problems and it would appear that they are having success, which, happily, is being reflected in increasing sales.

S P E C I F I C A T I O N	
MODEL/TYPE	LOTUS EXCEL
ENGINE	4-CYL, 2,174CC, SOHC
HORSEPOWER	160BHP @ 6,500RPM
TRANSMISSION	5-SPEED MANUAL
CHASSIS	STEEL BACKBONE
BRAKES	4-WHEEL DISC
TOP SPEED	134MPH
ACCELERATION 0–60MPH	7 SECS
PRODUCTION SPAN	1984 →

A subtle rounding out of the Lotus Excel's extremities has given looks to match the car's performance from the neat 16-valve four-cylinder engine *(opposite bottom)*. The four-seater Lotus is big but not heavy, quick but easily handled and exclusive but not unattainable.

152 MPH

LOTUS ESPRIT TURBO

The 1985 Esprit Turbo has a number of all-new features, in particular a new chassis and revised front suspension, as well as new brakes, electrics, tyres and body and trim details. The chassis now has an eight-year anti-corrosion warranty.

The heart of the Turbo is the mid-mounted 910 2.2-litre four-cylinder engine with four valves per cylinder. The turbocharger blows through two Dellorto carburettors which are mounted as close as possible to the intake manifold so that turbo-lag is virtually eliminated. Power of 210bhp is delivered at 6,500rpm, giving the car a top speed of 152mph. Acceleration from zero to 100mph takes an astonishing 14.6 seconds. Remarkable fuel economy bears out the high efficiency of this engine, being quoted as 24.1mpg at a steady 75mph.

This extraordinary car is given one of the most dramatic shapes by the Italian stylist Giugiaro and like so many of his best designs for fast cars it looks to be travelling fast even when standing still. For two people (with only a small amount of luggage) it is one of the best ways of covering long distances at very high speeds in comfort and safety.

LOTUS

S P E C I F I C A T I O N	
MODEL/TYPE	LOTUS ESPRIT TURBO
ENGINE	4-CYL, 2,174CC, SOHC
HORSEPOWER	210BHP @ 6,500RPM
TRANSMISSION	5-SPEED MANUAL
CHASSIS	STEEL BACKBONE
BRAKES	4-WHEEL DISC
TOP SPEED	152MPH
ACCELERATION 0–60MPH	5.5 SECS
PRODUCTION SPAN	1980 →

The mid-engined Lotus Esprit Turbo amply demonstrates Lotus's late founder Colin Chapman's philosophy of 'no bloody compromise'. If you want this kind of performance you must travel light and if you don't want to hear the engine noise, buy a bike.

LOTUS ETNA

In October 1984 Lotus announced their new 'Concept' car, called the Etna. This could be, indeed should be, the Lotus standard-bearer to take them into the 1990s. Styled by Giugiaro at Ital Design, it has one of the cleanest, most dashing body shapes ever seen on a British car. Slightly larger than the current Esprit model, it is hoped that it will be very little heavier than that car in spite of having the exciting new Lotus V8 engine installed. It is expected that it will cost £35,000 in Britain when in production. The whole car promises to be state-of-the-art in super-fast car construction and performance and other fast car makers will have to watch out once this car gets into the showrooms.

The heart of the Etna will be the new V8 engine. This 4-litre unit develops 340bhp now, with much more to come if the care in development that Lotus is lavishing upon it is anything to go by. This engine will be the jewel in the crown of the remarkable new Lotus, but it looks as if it will be 1987 before the first production cars come off the Hethel production lines.

S P E C I F I C A T I O N	
MODEL/TYPE	LOTUS ETNA
ENGINE	V8, 4,000CC, DOHC
HORSEPOWER	340BHP @ 6,500RPM
TRANSMISSION	5-SPEED MANUAL
CHASSIS	STEEL BACKBONE
BRAKES	4-WHEEL DISC
TOP SPEED	182MPH
ACCELERATION 0–100MPH	10.6 SECS
PRODUCTION SPAN	1987 →

Lotus's next-generation supercar, the Giugiaro-styled V8-powered Etna, caused a sensation when it was unveiled in prototype form in 1984—and not surprisingly so. It is by far the most sophisticated Lotus to date and by far the quickest ever for the road.

S P E C I F I C A T I O N	
MODEL/TYPE	TVR 390SE
ENGINE	V8, 3,900CC
HORSEPOWER	275BHP @ 5,500RPM
TRANSMISSION	5-SPEED MANUAL
CHASSIS	STEEL BACKBONE
BRAKES	4-WHEEL DISC
TOP SPEED	150MPH
ACCELERATION 0–60MPH	5 SECS
PRODUCTION SPAN	1984 →

TVR 390SE

Finally for this British section, I have chosen one model from the three car TVR range because it encompasses all that is excellent about this small, high quality car maker. The TVR 390SE is a front-engined, rear-wheel-drive sports coupé using a separate steel chassis and a glass-reinforced plastic moulded body. Like those on the Lotus cars, this body is made in two halves, which are bonded along the waistline in the finishing process. The chassis is a multi-tubular steel backbone, very carefully protected against corrosion and with all-independent suspension. Braking is by ventilated disc units all round and rack and pinion steering is used. The 390SE rides on 225/50 VR 15 tyres, on alloy wheels. The 3,900cc V8 engine, derived from the Rover Vitesse unit, develops 275bhp at 5,500rpm and will whisk the TVR to over 150mph and from rest to 60mph in just 5 seconds, which puts it firmly in the supercar league. The engine uses Lucas electronic fuel injection and gives the car an average fuel consumption of between 20 and 25mpg.

In addition to the coupé, the 390SE can be ordered in convertible trim, although to my eyes the coupé is the better looking car. Priced at £19,700 in Britain, the TVR 390SE is a worthy competitor to several other fast cars and has the added advantage of being made by a company which takes great pride in its customer relations.

Hand-built by humans, not hand-built by robots, in a small factory in the seaside funfair town of Blackpool; the TVR 390iSE will out-accelerate virtually any production car in the world and offers a brand of exclusivity that more famous marques somehow lack.

JAPAN

Until recent years, the Japanese auto industry has concentrated mainly on producing transportation for millions of buyers world-wide who require no more than reliable, inexpensive cars. Their performance cars could be counted on the fingers of less than one hand but in the last four or five years that has begun to change and now there are several very worthy vehicles coming out of Japanese factories that, on their own merits, qualify for a place in this book.

A car that can probably make an honest claim to having been the first complete Japanese performance car must be the Datsun 240Z. The trouble with the 240Z is that the makers, Nissan, were so impressed by their success in the North American market that they fell into the trap of making regular changes to the car along the lines of giving it more comfort, more chromium plating, more styling features, more weight, more engine and more gadgets. All of that simply added more bulk to the whole car and gradually eroded the vehicle's initially impressive performance, making the last of the line, the 280ZX, into a caricature of the original (a pig's ear out of a near silk purse).

Japanese industry, however, whatever the product, has the flexibility and the long-range commercial vision to take heed of past mistakes and it also has the money to put them right, even if that means starting with a clean sheet of paper. There are now several Japanese cars that deserve close scrutiny.

S P E C I F I C A T I O N	
MODEL/TYPE	NISSAN 300ZX TURBO
ENGINE	V6, 2,960CC, OHC, TURBO
HORSEPOWER	228BHP @ 5,400RPM
TRANSMISSION	5-SPEED MANUAL
CHASSIS	STEEL MONOCOQUE
BRAKES	4-WHEEL DISC
TOP SPEED	141MPH
ACCELERATION 0–60MPH	7.2 SECS
PRODUCTION SPAN	1984 →

NISSAN 300ZX TURBO

As Nissan were the first mass producer of a fast Japanese car it is only right that they should start off this chapter with their latest 300ZX Turbo. The car's makers claim a top speed of 141mph and 0–60mph in 7.2 seconds, while the 300ZX Turbo also has a reasonable fuel consumption figure of 21.5mpg. Those are the bare facts but there is more to any car than just those, and it is interesting to see that the 300ZX shapes up pretty well on the road.

The car's clean shape is broken only by the necessary bonnet top bulge and a 'sameness' about its overall styling; aerodynamic considerations now play such a significant part in any car's appearance that they just have to be overlooked. The 2.96-litre V6 engine is boosted by a Garrett turbocharger to give 228bhp at 5,400rpm. Electronic fuel injection and ignition are fitted to aid the splendid flexibility which is one of the V6's best features.

On driving off in the 300ZX Turbo, the comfort and refinement are most noticeable. Noise insulation is good but not so good is the rather too soft ride, an obvious sop to a part of the American market that the car could well do without. At high speeds there is too much wind noise for real comfort.

Roadholding is uniformly good and the car has no particularly bad habits so long as its understeering tendency is kept in mind. Slow in and fast out is the watchword when driving the 300ZX Turbo fast through corners. Wet road behaviour is not so good, mainly because of the lack of real grip from the Japanese-made 205/55 VR 16 Dunlop tyres, which let go far too early for any driver's peace of mind. The dampers have a dash adjustable control which allows the driver to select either soft, normal or firm settings. Set on 'firm', the car becomes too nervous and could give a driver problems if driven too fast on twisty roads, so most people stay with the 'soft' setting, which suits the car's American nature much more. The brakes, discs all round, are well up to the task of stopping the 300ZX Turbo at

S P E C I F I C A T I O N	
MODEL/TYPE	NISSAN SILVIA TURBO
ENGINE	4-CYL, 1,809CC, TURBO
HORSEPOWER	135BHP @ 6,000RPM
TRANSMISSION	5-SP/3-SP AUTO
CHASSIS	STEEL MONOCOQUE
BRAKES	4-WHEEL DISC
TOP SPEED	126MPH
ACCELERATION 0–60MPH	8.9 SECS
PRODUCTION SPAN	1984 →

all the speeds that it is capable of.

At nearly twice the price of a Ford Capri 2.8 Injection Special the Nissan is not twice as good a car and on this basis, at least, does not represent good value for money.

NISSAN SILVIA TURBO

The smaller sister car to the 300ZX Turbo is much more in the cast of a European sports coupé. This is the Nissan Silvia Turbo ZX. It uses a turbocharged 1.8-litre overhead-cam engine, which delivers 135bhp and a claimed top speed of 126mph, plus the benefits of engine efficiency revealed by an excellent fuel economy figure of 44mpg at 65mph.

For lazy drivers, the Silvia can be ordered with a three-speed plus overdrive top automatic gearbox but the manual five-speed 'box is really too good to pass up. With all-round independent suspension, rack-and-pinion steering and four-wheel disc brakes, the chassis is well equipped to handle the engine's fine performance. The Silvia is better balanced than the 300ZX Turbo, and has an outstanding ability to cover the miles fast and safely. Its styling is perhaps just a little too bland, even anonymous, to be a head-turner, but it is clean and aerodynamically stable. The car is a pleasure to drive when carrying just two people and their luggage but as a 2+2 it has only limited use for four adults. The Silvia Turbo ZX then, can be summed up as an efficient, fast coupé but bland to the point of being characterless.

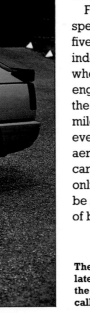

The Nissan 300ZX Turbo is the latest in a line which started with the 240Z—when Nissan still called its cars Datsuns—and it is the best in the series since the classic original. The Nissan Silvia Turbo is Nissan's alternative performance car.

COLT STARION

The Mitsubishi Colt Starion is another Japanese performance coupé which uses the assistance of a turbocharger to boost its power. This model has a 2-litre engine, rather smaller than the norm for this size of car, but the latest model utilizes all the latest turbo technology to extract an excellent 168bhp at 5,500rpm, giving the Starion a claimed top speed of 137mph. Acceleration from zero to 62mph is equally impressive, at just 7.6 seconds.

Spoilers front and rear aid aerodynamics and combat lift at speed but do not detract from the clean shape of the car, especially now that it has a clean bonnet top, without the previous power bulge. The Starion's steering is different from that of other Japanese fast cars (with the one exception of the Mazda RX-7) in being of recirculating-ball type. This in a Japanese application usually means a deadness in the straight ahead position and a certain looseness in feel. However, like BMW, Mitsubishi have produced a system using this method that is very close to being as good as a rack and pinion set-up. A five-speed manual gearbox is standard with ratios that complement the blown four-cylinder engine's power output extremely well.

The Starion also has a new door hinge design that is double jointed and allows a wider opening, making for easier entry and exit. The driving compartment is very fully equipped, with good seats, an equally good driving position with all controls to hand and vision out is as good as that in any other fast coupé, and better than some.

On the road the Starion is great fun, yet not tiring to drive for long distances. Wind noise is unusually low, complementing the easy nature of the car. At 100mph, with less than 4,000rpm on the tachometer, the car is uncanny, it is *so* quiet. With its 16.5-gallon fuel tank and an average consumption of around 25mpg, the Starion can really cover the miles between refuelling and at least 350 miles per tank is normal. Because of the size of the fuel tank, however, luggage space is rather more limited than in other coupés.

Handling is good, being firm and slightly choppy as the all-round MacPherson strut-type suspension is more biased to handling than to ride comfort and in my opinion that is justified by the competent manner of its going. The brakes are quite simply superb — they stopped the car from all speeds without any drama at all and are one of the best features of the car (although the interior is also a feature to be commented upon, as it is to a very high standard, in fit and finish and in its ergonomics which allow the driver and passenger to enjoy the car to the maximum).

Unlike many Japanese cars which I find rather bland, the Starion has real character, is enormous fun to use and is well enough made to represent a long term investment in a fast car.

COLT

S P E C I F I C A T I O N	
MODEL/TYPE	COLT STARION
ENGINE	4-CYL, 1,987CC, TURBO
HORSEPOWER	168BHP @ 5,500RPM
TRANSMISSION	5-SPEED MANUAL
CHASSIS	STEEL MONOCOQUE
BRAKES	4-WHEEL DISC
TOP SPEED	137MPH
ACCELERATION 0–62MPH	7.6 SECS
PRODUCTION SPAN	1983 →

Colt's considerable experience—and success—in production racing is evidenced by the company's reputation for building rapid and rugged cars for the road, from small turbo hatchbacks to this top-of-the-range Starion coupé.

S P E C I F I C A T I O N	
MODEL/TYPE	TOYOTA CELICA SUPRA
ENGINE	6-CYL, 2,759CC, SOHC
HORSEPOWER	168BHP @ 5,600RPM
TRANSMISSION	5-SPEED MANUAL
CHASSIS	STEEL MONOCOQUE
BRAKES	4-WHEEL DISC
TOP SPEED	136MPH
ACCELERATION 0–60MPH	8.3 SECS
PRODUCTION SPAN	1984 →

Toyota have made very great steps in the last three years to uprate their 'Old man' image. To this end they have been improving several of their cars and as recently as January 1985 they introduced two new fast models that should appeal to fast car fans world-wide.

TOYOTA CELICA SUPRA

The Celica Supra 2.8i has been updated, and is interesting in that in the suspension department it now displays the first results of the Toyota/Lotus partnership.

First, however, to the engine, which is a classic 2,759cc twin-cam straight-six driving the rear axle via a five-speed gearbox. It produces 168bhp at 5,600rpm using electronic fuel injection. Brakes are ventilated discs at both front and rear, with servo-assistance. Steering is by an excellent power-assisted rack-and-pinion system. These features, plus the use of 225/60VR 14 tyres and the Lotus-inspired changes to the chassis, make for a car that although lacking the power of its turbocharged rivals can happily stay with them during high speed cross-country travel.

The engine and transmission are a delight. Not having turbo-boost means not having any turbo-lag and the spread of engine power is such that the Supra is more relaxing to drive in all conditions of road, traffic and weather than most. Fit and finish are first-rate and although there is much evidence of plastic in the interior, it is very tastefully done and doesn't detract too much. With a top speed of 136mph and a time of 8.3 seconds for 0–60mph, the Supra is certainly no slouch and it is also very fine value for money.

The splendid mid-engined Toyota MR2 (top) is one of the most exciting new cars for many years for lovers of the fast car and with the more conventional but even faster Celica Supra (right), offers proof positive that the world's biggest motor manufacturer still believes in performance.

S P E C I F I C A T I O N	
MODEL/TYPE	TOYOTA MR2
ENGINE	4-CYL, 1,587CC, DOHC
HORSEPOWER	122BHP @ 6,600RPM
TRANSMISSION	5-SPEED MANUAL
CHASSIS	STEEL MONOCOQUE
BRAKES	4-WHEEL DISC
TOP SPEED	125MPH
ACCELERATION 0–60MPH	8.1 SECS
PRODUCTION SPAN	1985 →

TOYOTA MR2

The very latest in Toyota's fast car line-up is the long awaited MR2 sports coupé. This mid-engined device was announced to the British press in Portugal in January 1985, on a test route that was not in any way selected to pamper the cars but was capable of highlighting the smallest deficiency in their behaviour. After some time thrashing the MR2 around the mountains I was left with the impression, the firm impression, that with this car Toyota have a winner.

The car uses what must be the best mass-produced four-cylinder engine available in the world today, the twin-cam 4A-GE unit of 1,587cc capacity, which produces 122bhp at 6,600rpm and drives through a five-speed gearbox and transaxle arrangement. The MR2 will reach a top speed of 125mph and accelerate to 60mph from rest in 8.1 seconds. At a constant 75mph it has excellent 36.7mpg fuel economy. The electronic fuel-injection system gives instant starting, fast cold drive-away and superb response at all engine speeds, so good as to make the five-speed gearbox almost redundant!

I found just two small points of criticism to mention after driving the car. Firstly, the fuel tank is too small at only nine gallons, it really should be at least half as big again, and secondly the interior for someone of my (largish) size was just a little cramped. For two average-sized people wanting to cover long distances fast, however, with a reasonable luggage carrying capacity, the MR2 is superb. Steering, brakes, stability at speed, driving position, controls, finish, are all simply marvellous. In the vast quantities that Toyota are capable of making, the MR2 must be a distinct thorn in the side of many other fast coupé manufacturers the world over — and that is irrespective of any price considerations. It is certainly one of the best fast car bargains available today.

TOYOTA COROLLA GT

A very brief mention must be made here of the sister car to the MR2, the Corolla GT. Designed to compete with all the other fast hatchback models flooding onto today's market, the Corolla GT has the same superb 16-valve 1,587cc engine as the MR2 but front-mounted and driving the front wheels. Unlike the MR2 it is a genuine four-seater with all four sitting much higher off the ground. Disc brakes all round, rack-and-pinion steering, alloy wheels and 186/60HR 14 tyres and all-independent suspension with gas-filled dampers give the GT performance that enables it to challenge the mighty VW Golf GTi. Because of the higher seating position and the better visibility I actually prefer it to the MR2, and its low price, cheaper than a Volkswagen Golf GTi, makes it particularly competitive, a very fine car.

S P E C I F I C A T I O N	
MODEL/TYPE	TOYOTA COROLLA GT
ENGINE	4-CYL, 1,587CC, DOHC
HORSEPOWER	122BHP @ 6,600RPM
TRANSMISSION	5-SPEED MANUAL
CHASSIS	STEEL MONOCOQUE
BRAKES	4-WHEEL DISC
TOP SPEED	125MPH
ACCELERATION 0–60MPH	8.7 SECS
PRODUCTION SPAN	1984 →

TOYOTA

Sharing the same basic
powertrain as the new mid-
engined MR2, the 125mph Corolla
GT finally lays to rest Toyota's
formerly well-deserved image as
a maker of very ordinary
motorcars.

MAZDA

MAZDA/ELFORD RX-7T

I have left the Mazda RX-7 Turbo till last, because the basic RX-7 is now eight years old, although it has been uprated annually to keep pace with other similar coupés. Above all though, it is its use of a Wankel rotary engine that sets the RX-7 apart from so many other fast cars and gives the car its very special personality.

The latest in the line, the RX-7 Turbo, has been available, although only in Japan, for some months now and a factory-approved turbo conversion made by the Elford Engineering Company in Great Britain has been available in Europe since 1983. The 'official' car is listed as the GT-X model, and features a Hitachi-made turbo unit, the 18S-BM model. It generates a 27% increase in horsepower over the standard car's 135bhp. All the drivetrain components have been strengthened to handle this increase but everything else on the car remains the same. Eight-position adjustable dampers are fitted but they are not very convenient to adjust! A speed-variable steering mechanism is fitted and works very well.

The RX-7 GT-X rides on 205/60VR 14 tyres, which contribute a great deal to the car's roadholding capabilities. The all-round disc brakes have been increased in diameter but just about everything else is standard.

With its 7,500rpm limit, the RX-7 GT-X is a very fast car, but the engine has to reach at least 3,000rpm before any real power is forthcoming. Once spinning it will take the car up to, and a little beyond, 140mph but at these speeds the recirculating-ball steering is rather too light and lacking in feel for comfort. The car has benefitted from this extra power but it is not really enough to prevent many potential buyers discarding any thoughts of buying the Mazda in favour of more modern cars of superior performance. Nothing, however, can take the place of the superb rotary engine, which has been described by one of America's foremost rotary experts as 'absolutely bullet-proof!'.

The Elford Engineering version of the RX-7 with turbo power is just as well engineered as the factory car, and like that machine takes the RX-7 theme a giant step forward in the performance field. Quite simply, it is very fast (with a top speed of over 130mph), very smooth, very reliable and, with the Elford-designed aerodynamic aids, looks great. It is also one of the best buys in the fast car market.

When Elford engineering adds a turbocharger to the already excellent rotary-engined Mazda RX-7, the result is a car with a unique personality and effortless performance.

S P E C I F I C A T I O N	
MODEL/TYPE	MAZDA/ELFORD RX-7T
ENGINE	ROTARY, 2,300CC, TURBO
HORSEPOWER	135BHP @ 6,000RPM
TRANSMISSION	5-SPEED MANUAL
CHASSIS	STEEL MONOCOQUE
BRAKES	4-WHEEL DISC
TOP SPEED	135MPH PLUS
ACCELERATION 0–60MPH	8 SECS
PRODUCTION SPAN	1983 →

MAZDA/ELFORD 929C-TURBO

Turbo power, again by courtesy of Elford, turns Mazda's rather dowdy 929 coupé into something altogether more interesting and individual—a Q-car in the finest tradition.

Elford have also turned their hand to the rather gutless Mazda 929 coupé, which shares the Wankel engine, giving it turbo-power and turning it into one of the best value-for-money four-seater cars in Europe. I have driven the first example of the converted car, trying it both with and without the turbo operating. The difference is astonishing. Without the turbo the car has a real struggle to get to 98mph, with the meagre 90bhp that is available from the four-cylinder single overhead cam engine. The Elford-Garrett T3 turbo changes all that to 135bhp at 5,800rpm. In making the car faster the extra power changes the function of the gearbox from a four-speed plus overdrive fifth, to something that feels much more like a close-ratio sports 'box. In top gear the car really benefits from the added engine power instead of struggling to maintain a fast cruising speed and will accelerate happily and rapidly up to its 127mph top speed with ease and hold it in the face of most gradients.

The turbo installation is neat and tidy, looking for all the world like a factory fitment. The rest of the car is equally good, a very comfortable four-seater with all the controls and instruments that any driver could wish for. Power-assisted steering and four-wheel disc brakes allow the car's performance to be exploited to the full. The car looks good and unlike so many other Japanese models it is both competent and full of character.

The cars that have featured in this chapter represent the cutting edge of a new wave of performance cars that will be coming out of Japan from now on. With their dedication, mass production backing and very keen appreciation of what the market wants, plus their policy of very competitive pricing, Japanese car makers are likely to become increasingly prominent in this once solely European field.

S P E C I F I C A T I O N	
MODEL/TYPE	MAZDA/Elford 929C TURBO
ENGINE	ROTARY-TURBO
HORSEPOWER	135BHP @ 5,800RPM
TRANSMISSION	5-SPEED MANUAL
CHASSIS	STEEL MONOCOQUE
BRAKES	4-WHEEL DISC
TOP SPEED	127MPH
ACCELERATION 0–60MPH	N/A
PRODUCTION SPAN	1984 →

MAZDA

CHEVROLET CORVETTE

Although it is no longer the fastest American car (that honour nowadays rests with the Chevrolet Camaro IROC-Z machine which is two or three mph faster) the Chevrolet Corvette is the longest-running sporty car still being produced in the USA. Real performance is again beginning to tempt American buyers and manufacturers and many very quick cars are likely to be announced in the USA in coming months.

The 'Vette was given a whole new suit of clothes two years ago but until the 1985 model appeared, it flattered only to deceive with production examples not living up to the pre-production demonstrator cars. Chevrolet took a tremendous battering from customers and other critics about the car and buckled down to putting all the points raised to rights. The 1985 Corvette, it is good to report, is all that the car should have been in the first place. The engine is the traditional pushrod 5,733cc V8, which, with fuel injection makes a lowly 230bhp at 4,000rpm, but torque is an excellent 330lb ft at 3,200rpm.

The new body shape has lost all the odd bumps and lumps that marred the previous model and now looks modern and up to date. The interior features a digital instrument layout (which is not as good as the old analogue), proper adjust-able seats, with leather as an optional covering, and a Delco-GM/Bose sound system that gives concert hall quality.

On the road the new 'Vette is tight and solid, where-as the 1984 model was a mass of squeaks and rattles. It goes very well and a top speed of over 150mph, with 0–60mph in 6 seconds is not hanging about by any standards. Roadholding is equally good but the brakes, while good in most circumstances, lack conviction at the limit. The Corvette will deliver an average of 16 miles from a US gallon of leadless gasoline. It may not have the very long term in-tegrity of, say, a Porsche 928S, but it is excellent value for money.

S P E C I F I C A T I O N	
MODEL/TYPE	CHEVROLET CORVETTE
ENGINE	V8, 5,733CC
HORSEPOWER	230BHP @ 4,000RPM
TRANSMISSION	4-SPEED AUTO
CHASSIS	STEEL FRAME/GRP BODY
BRAKES	4-WHEEL DISC
TOP SPEED	150MPH
ACCELERATION 0–100MPH	16.5 SECS
PRODUCTION SPAN	1985 →

American fast cars come and go but the Chevrolet Corvette goes on forever. The latest model of America's favourite sportscar continues an unbroken line going back to 1953, when General Motors took the plunge with a European-style roadster. Today's Corvette is a far cry from the original but the name still evokes magic.

FORD MERKUR XR4T-i

The Merkur is a Sierra-based coupé, a three-door hatchback with the 'biplane' rear spoiler. Its engine is a 2.3-litre, four-cylinder single overhead cam unit with a Garrett TO3B turbocharger and it gives 170bhp at 5,200rpm in manual gearbox form. It is front mounted and drives the rear wheels via a five-speed manual or Ford C3 automatic 'box. Suspension is fully independent and brakes are discs at the front and drums at the rear. Steering is by power-assisted rack-and-pinion. Alloy wheels carry 195/60HR 14 Pirelli P6 tyres. With the possible exception of the brakes (rear drums do not indicate a full commitment to high speed use), the whole design of the Merkur XR4Ti suggests the intention of the makers to provide the customer with a proper fast car. It will reach 125mph easily but no acceleration times are published.

FORD

S P E C I F I C A T I O N	
MODEL/TYPE	FORD MERKUR XR4T-i
ENGINE	4-CYL, 2,298CC TURBO
HORSEPOWER	170BHP @ 5,200RPM
TRANSMISSION	5-SP/3-SP AUTO
CHASSIS	STEEL MONOCOQUE
BRAKES	DISC FRONT, DRUM REAR
TOP SPEED	125MPH PLUS
ACCELERATION	N/A
PRODUCTION SPAN	1985 →

With the coming of the 'world car', Europe and America have shared more ideas than ever before. The Ford Merkur XR4Ti is the American incarnation of the Sierra, with a turbo for good measure.

FORD

FORD MUSTANG GT

The Ford Mustang has always had a reputation as a fast car even if that reputation has not always been justified. Now, after some years in the doldrums, two new Mustangs have been offered to American buyers and these Mustangs really do have a claim as performance cars. The Mustang GT and the SVO models are significantly different in the way they go about being fast cars but in the end that is what they both prove to be. The GT model has a 5-litre pushrod V8 engine that develops a very unstressed 210bhp. It drives through a five-speed gearbox that seems just a touch heavy in operation, to a solid rear axle which is located by coil springs and 'Quadra-Shock' suspension.

The Mustang GT rides on handsome alloy wheels of 15-in diameter and which carry P225/60VR 15 Goodyear Eagle tyres. These fine tyres contribute a great deal to the Mustang's handling and stable ride. The whole car is very solidly built, the interior is well trimmed and only the masking of some of the instrument faces spoils the overall good impression.

Brakes are again a disappointing mixture of disc front and drum rear but in today's American driving environment they prove to be adequate rather than inspiring. Power-assisted rack-and-pinion steering is used, and I found this to be excellent.

From a performance point of view the GT is really good. It has bags of acceleration and Ford claim it will exceed 130mph, which I have no reason to doubt, having driven it. The GT version of the Mustang theme represents the ultimate expression of the traditional big American V8 in a small, or at least compact, body, this time with decent brakes and good roadholding as well. The Ford GT is also available in convertible form and, unusually for an American car, it cannot be ordered with an automatic gearbox!

S P E C I F I C A T I O N	
MODEL/TYPE	FORD MUSTANG GT
ENGINE	V8, 5,000CC
HORSEPOWER	210BHP @ 4,400RPM
TRANSMISSION	5-SPEED MANUAL
CHASSIS	STEEL MONOCOQUE
BRAKES	DISC FRONT, DRUM REAR
TOP SPEED	125MPH
ACCELERATION 0–60MPH	N/A
PRODUCTION SPAN	1984 →

The original Mustang was one of Ford's major triumphs but the name was later used on some very ordinary cars. The latest Mustang GT goes some way to restoring some of the name's former reputation.

FORD MUSTANG SVO

The Ford SVO (Special Vehicles Operation) is the next step in the direction that American Fords are taking. It represents the hi-tech way of doing things, no more brute muscle as in the GT, but more of the subtler European-type approach, that is using turbochargers allied to relatively small engines, with digital electronic fuel-injection and ignition systems to produce the horsepower. In the case of the SVO, a 2.3-litre four-cylinder overhead cam engine and Garrett turbocharger produce 175bhp at 4,400rpm. The EEC-IV computer-controlled blower allows an infinitely variable boost up to an unusually high 14psi.

The SVO's suspension has the excellent Koni dampers installed. Power-assisted rack-and-pinion steering is fitted and 16 × 7in cast alloy wheels carry P225/50VR 16 Goodyear tyres. This complete package gives the car very good handling and ride qualities. I have driven the car for considerable distances on freeways and minor roads of a very twisty nature and at all speeds the SVO stuck to the road as though it was glued there! The handling in corners, fast and slow, was excellent, supplemented by the fine steering. The brakes, unlike those on the GT are ventilated discs at the front and rear, and power-assisted, of course.

A 200% Porsche fan who I have known for some years surprised me with his enthusiasm for the SVO. He likes the car so much that he has sold his current Porsche and ordered one of these very special Fords. He calls it the best all-round, value car in America today, and he cannot wait to take delivery of it!

Now that US manufacturers have rediscovered performance and found that it still sells, it seems that the next few months will produce a great many really quick, interesting cars from the USA; in particular, you might watch out for the results of the Ford Saturn project. It will be spectacular!

S P E C I F I C A T I O N	
MODEL/TYPE	FORD MUSTANG SVO
ENGINE	4-CYL, 2,300CC, TURBO
HORSEPOWER	175BHP @ 4,400RPM
TRANSMISSION	5-SPEED MANUAL
CHASSIS	STEEL MONOCOQUE
BRAKES	4-WHEEL DISC
TOP SPEED	OVER 125MPH
ACCELERATION 0–60MPH	7.76 SECS
PRODUCTION SPAN	1984 →

FORD

The cockpit (*above*) of the Ford
Mustang SVO (*left*) shows
America's growing acceptance of
the more restrained interior
styling of European cars—
especially sporting models.

FRANCE & SWEDEN

CITROEN CX25 GTi-TURBO

The French have been making fast cars for as long as anyone else but for some time now they haven't had more than one or two really quick, specialist-built cars, such as the Facel Vega or the short-lived Monica. Now they have two excellent fast machines, one a normal production car, the Citroën GTi Turbo and the other a homologation special, the Peugeot 205 Turbo-16, both of which are genuine over-125mph cars.

Citroën claim that their CX GTi Turbo can reach 136mph and I for one am certainly not inclined to disbelieve them, in fact I suspect that if anything they are being rather conservative in this assertion. It has been reported that the CX's turbo installation is one of the very best available today. It gives the venerable 2.5-litre four-cylinder engine a whole new lease of life.

A new rear spoiler serves to maintain a decent drag figure of 0.36 and this plus the increased urge of the engine, up from 138bhp to 168bhp with the Garrett turbo and Bosch fuel injection, give the car its new high speed image. Acceleration too is good for such a big car, at only 8.6 seconds for zero to 60mph.

All the usual CX advantages are still present, including a long-legged ability to eat up the motorway miles, the excellent, but just a little too sensitive, all-round disc braking system, which makes light of stopping the 3,053lb car from any speed, the very comfortable interior and the slightly 'odd-ball' instrumentation and controls. Like all previous Citroëns it is not really a car to jump into and drive off without thinking. A Citroën rewards its driver if he or she takes the time to get to know the car and, once acquired, the Citroën addiction is very hard to get rid of.

S P E C I F I C A T I O N	
MODEL/TYPE	CITROEN CX25 GTi-TURBO
ENGINE	4-CYL, 2,500CC TURBO
HORSEPOWER	168BHP @ 5,000RPM
TRANSMISSION	5-SPEED MANUAL
CHASSIS	STEEL MONOCOQUE
BRAKES	4-WHEEL DISC
TOP SPEED	136MPH
ACCELERATION 0–60MPH	8.6 SECS
PRODUCTION SPAN	1984 →

It may not be the most obvious of sporting cars but the front-wheel-drive Citroën CX25GTi Turbo shows that the makers of the 2CV have not forgotten the opposite end of the market. The Turbo's top speed is almost exactly double that of the much loved *deux-chevaux*!

PEUGEOT

S P E C I F I C A T I O N	
MODEL/TYPE	PEUGEOT 205 TURBO 16
ENGINE	4-CYL, 1,775CC, TURBO
HORSEPOWER	200BHP @ 7,250RPM
TRANSMISSION	5-SPEED MANUAL
CHASSIS	MONOCOQUE/TUBULAR
BRAKES	4-WHEEL DISC
TOP SPEED	130MPH PLUS
ACCELERATION 0–60MPH	5.8 SECS
PRODUCTION SPAN	1984 →

PEUGEOT 205 TURBO 16

When the Peugeot 205 model range was announced, early in 1983, it created a sensation. The 205 had up-to-date styling, fine performance, very good ride and handling and it had what no other Peugeot had had before, it had chic — a charm that drew the customers into Peugeot dealerships in their thousands. The company has had to increase production rates of the car several times over in the two years since then to meet the demand. With their super GTi model the demand shot up again with the 205, Peugeot could do no wrong.

The company also went rallying, but with a car that was even more outstanding: the 205 turbocharged 16-valve-engined, four-wheel-drive machine. They won rallies, including the 1985 Monte Carlo, in which they took first, third and fifth places overall. To be able to enter this extraordinary car in international competition Peugeot had to build at least 200 customer examples, which they have done, and they have sold every available car.

On seeing the car for the first time it is obvious even to the uninitiated that this is a racer. It could be nothing else, with its big wheels, the air intake for the mid-mounted engine, the spoilers — they all go to state that this is not a normal drive-to-the-station commuter car. The 1,775cc engine uses four valves per cylinder and is blown by an intercooled German-made KKK turbocharger. It churns out 200bhp at 7,250rpm and there is little real power under 3,000rpm but once the tachometer needle hits 4,000rpm things really start to happen. If it were not for the four-wheel-drive arrangement the car would be difficult to control.

Driving this competition-inspired vehicle calls for firm and positive action on the part of the driver, the Peugeot has to be made to obey directions and this is no car to pussyfoot around, it has to be dominated. There is little, if any, luggage room in the car, it is noisy and can be tiring to drive far, but the *fun* factor is sky-high.

The Peugeot 205 Turbo 16 in
works competition guise ended
the Audi Quattro's near monopoly
of rally wins in 1984 and the
model is also now available as a
rather special road car.

SPECIFICATION	
MODEL/TYPE	SAAB 9000T
ENGINE	4-CYL, 1,985CC, DOHC
HORSEPOWER	175BHP @ 5,500RPM
TRANSMISSION	5-SPEED MANUAL
CHASSIS	STEEL MONOCOQUE
BRAKES	4-WHEEL DISC
TOP SPEED	130MPH
ACCELERATION 0–60MPH	8.2 SECS
PRODUCTION SPAN	1985

SAAB 9000T

Apart from their rally cars, Saab have never had a reputation for building wild, fast, ultra-exciting vehicles. Sensible — yes; functional — yes; very well made — yes; but *not* cars that get the blood boiling, more cars of the head than of the heart. With Saab's new 900 16S and 9000 models however, there could well be a change in the wind.

The 9000's styling has none of that 'Look at Me, I'm a Super Car' gimmickry that others go for. It is a sober, functional shape, with enormous interior space, a well laid out set of instruments and controls to aid the driver at his task and, under the bonnet, all the latest sophistication to be expected of a fourth generation turbo-car.

It undoubtedly goes; a factory claim of over 135mph has been confirmed in many road-tests. It has stability at speed, it has excellent roadholding and ride qualities, it shows all the effort put into it after ten years of painstaking research and development. The 1,985cc four-cylinder engine has four valves per cylinder and double overhead cams. The inter-cooled turbo unit produces a full 175bhp but there is a problem, or rather two problems with the 9000. Its steering is lacking in feel, which doesn't help the strong understeering nature of the chassis, and there is a disconcerting 'On-Off' character in the engine's power delivery. Both of these items can make it difficult to drive the 9000 fast in the dry and very difficult in the wet. Power delivery goes from almost nothing to full blast in a spread of only 500rpm. At 2,500rpm there is little in the way of real power but by 3,000rpm the turbo is well into its work.

Maybe the answer to the steering response lies in the tyre size, because they do appear to be on the narrow side, and compared to, say, an Audi 2005T, the Saab 9000 is a little deficient in the way it puts its 175bhp down on the road. By the time it is in the dealers' showrooms these small deficiencies will undoubtedly be sorted out.

The attractive Saab 9000 saloon features the first all-new bodyshape from the Swedish manufacturer for several years and much new engineering under the skin further enhances Saab's considerable reputation for solid sporting performance.

Index